Praise for *Europe's Decline and Fall*

'Richard Youngs has produced a passionate but clear-headed analysis of Europe's shrinking status and stature in world affairs. Sarkozy, Merkel and Tusk, as well as MEPs and the Brussels bigwigs, should read, reflect and react to this wake-up call to reverse Europe's decline before it is too late.'

– Rt. Hon. Dr. Denis MacShane MP, Britain's longest serving Europe minister

'Richard Youngs is comprehensive in his analysis of the EU's failure to become a more effective global power. But he also comes up with original proposals for improving the EU's performance. He urges the EU to spend less time demanding that other countries should adopt its technical standards and follow its bureaucratic procedures. Instead, Youngs argues convincingly that Europe's leaders should do more to uphold liberal values around the world.'

– Charles Grant, director, Centre for European Reform

'As the world faces the biggest geopolitical upheaval for two centuries, a frightened Europe is hiding under the bedcovers. Richard Youngs makes a compelling case for the EU to climb out from beneath the duvet and shape its own destiny in the new world order.'

– Philip Stephens, associate editor and chief political commentator, *Financial Times*

EUROPE'S DECLINE AND FALL

AND FALL

THE STRUGGLE AGAINST GLOBAL IRRELEVANCE

Richard Youngs

P

PROFILE BOOKS

First published in Great Britain in 2010 by
Profile Books Ltd
3A Exmouth House
Pine Street
London EC1R 0JH
www.profilebooks.com

Typeset in Minion by MacGuru Ltd
info@macguru.org.uk
Printed and bound in Britain by
CPI Bookmarque, Croydon, Surrey

Mixed Sources
Product group from well-managed
forests and other controlled sources
www.fsc.org Cert no. TT-COC-002227
© 1996 Forest Stewardship Council

Contents

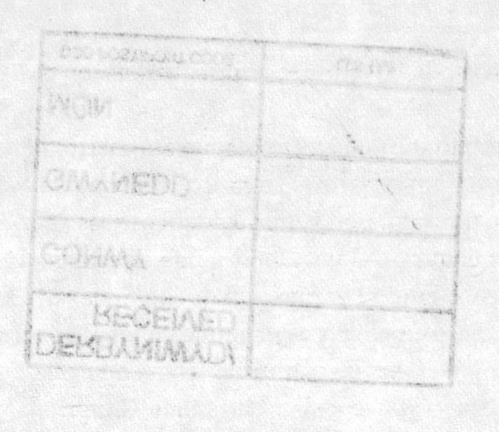

Preface

A decade ago Asian countries were wracked by financial crisis, at a time when the West was enjoying buoyant economic growth. Feeling that international support was unavailable on favourable conditions, these Asian states then spent a decade building up their own reserves as a system of self-assurance. Today East Asia, combined with oil-producing states, sits on surpluses of $8 trillion, while the eurozone and the USA have together run up $6 trillion worth of debt. Quite a dramatic turning of the tables – and indicative of the shift in power away from the West.

Preparation for this book began when the contours of Europe's decline were just beginning to sharpen into relief. By the time its writing was concluded, incipient concern had mutated into something approaching panic. This is not a book specifically about the crisis that has afflicted the euro during 2010 and which seems to have cracked the very pillars of solidarity underpinning the European Union. Yet this crisis is certainly one manifestation among several of the challenging trends which European governments now confront as they seek to grapple with a post-Western world. The turmoil associated with efforts to save the euro has brought to the surface the underlying magnitude of Europe's impending decline.

It is striking how much written comment and discussion

on the conference circuit still focuses on the apparent surprise factor in how far non-Western powers have come to rival the EU and the USA across a whole range of indicators. But this is no longer a novelty. We talk of 'emerging' powers which seem, in fact, to have very thoroughly 'emerged' already. It is time to stop simply expressing amazement at the diffusion of international influence among multiple centres of power. The debate must move on to a more systematic treatment of the question: what do we do about it? Several possible routes present themselves; which is the most advisable?

The route on which the EU (understood in this book as European governments acting both individually and collectively through European institutions) is tentatively setting out to temper the impact of its relative decline is the wrong one. Options are being followed according to a mistaken mindset that underlies thinking on economic, strategic, diplomatic and identity policies. The book suggests a series of guidelines to correct such misdirection. These invite the EU to be more open, internationalist and universal in its values.

The book's critique is presented in stark terms. Some may feel overly stark. But such a tone is part of its purpose. Timothy Garton Ash has pleaded: 'Europe, wake up!'[1] This book enters into the spirit of this injunction. It is always easy to add caveats, nuance and caution to any argument. For each area of criticism, some positive element of EU policy could be identified. But if Europe must be shaken from its

---

1   Timothy Garton Ash, 'Europe is sleepwalking to decline. We need a Churchill to wake it up', *Guardian*, 19 May 2010.

slumber, its dilemma and errors need to be painted in bold colours.

This is not an academic tome. For those seeking a more measured account that situates its analysis within ongoing scholarly debates, a list of the author's academic references, from which this volume draws, is supplied in the Appendix. Inspiration has been provided by some of the perceptive and stirring comment and analysis that has begun to appear on the subject of how Europe should manage its impending decline. The aim is to harness such analysis of separate parts of the jigsaw puzzle of decline and combine them into a comprehensive treatment of the topic that encompasses economic, political, strategic and identity-related issues. At the time of writing the outcome of the euro crisis is still uncertain, but it needs to be stressed that there are longer-term trends and challenges that lie beyond the question of how easily Europe's immediate financial instability can be halted.

I write these lines sitting in Seoul attending a meeting on Korea's preparations to chair the G20: a day squirming in discomfort as diplomats and analysts from Asia, Africa and Latin America constantly lambast Europeans for being the obstacle to equitable reform of international institutions and the restoration of financial stability. Referring to EU ideas for reforms within the G20, the representative of one developing country snorts dismissively: considering what you Europeans have just done to the global economy, your failure to deliver on promises, your narrow-minded clinging to over-representation in global bodies, why should we trust you? Not an atypical tone of seminar debate these days. Given the hope initially invested in the EU's common foreign policy, it is difficult not to lament: 'what a falling off was there'.[2] Europe still has the capacities to turn this situation around; but the time available for doing so is not limitless.

August 2010

---

2   William Shakespeare, *Hamlet*, Act 1, Scene 5.

1
Responding to decline

> 'It seems not unlikely that, during the next few centuries,
> civilisation, if it survives, will have greater diversity than it has
> had since the Renaissance. I think that if we are able to feel at
> home in the world … we shall have to admit Asia to equality
> in our thoughts, not only politically but culturally. What
> changes this will bring, I do not know, but I am convinced that
> they will be profound.'
>
> Bertrand Russell, History of Western Philosophy, 1946[1]

The cards appear well stacked. The die of European decline is cast. The shift in power from West to East has been exhaustively foretold. Pundits regularly point out that several centuries of Western dominance are drawing to an end. No longer will European nations play such a powerful role in determining the nature of the international system. No longer will they enjoy the same sway over the political values that prevail across the world, the principles that govern global politics, the shape of the international trading system or the outcome of bargaining over security, environmental

---

1   Bertrand Russell, *History of Western Philosophy*, 2004 edn, Routledge, London, 1946, p. 373.

and energy challenges. The flame of European power flickers more dimly. Europe's international shadow shortens.

Financial crisis has been followed by a sovereign debt crisis. In 2010 the EU has faced its most serious internal disarray for many decades, as governments have struggled to save the euro. Some of the basic pillars of EU unity are in peril. Far from designing proactive strategies for preserving global influence, European governments are scrambling to prevent the whole EU project collapsing. While governments focus on the immediate domestic imperatives of the economic crisis, the euro crisis itself reflects the broader challenge of underlying international decline. It forces many European governments to seek international credit, as emerging economies sit on growing piles of surplus reserves. China and the Gulf states in turn seek maximum advantage from pumping liquidity back into crisis-hit Western economies – although they also suffer now from having overextended their assets in debtor countries.

And hardly a day goes by without the headlines also bringing other examples of the gathering challenge to Western power. Emerging powers group together successfully to resist a European or US proposal in international trade negotiations. The 'global South' restricts the scope of international peacekeeping operations aimed at quelling a particular civil conflict. Non-Western states coordinate joint defence operations. Non-Western investment pours into a country whose human rights record attracts Western opprobrium. An apparently unassailable populist leader ridicules the idea that 'Western' values of democracy and liberal rights are universal. Western NGOs are evicted by an authoritarian regime no longer willing to tolerate their activities. An important energy-producing country threatens to shut down gas supplies in the midst of a harsh winter. Climate change talks hit another barrier as developing countries object to Western strictures. All these are now familiar stories in the daily coverage of international events.

Much has been written on the checking of US pre-eminence. Experts were pondering more than two decades ago what would come 'after American hegemony'. Analysts in the USA have long debated the 'end of the unipolar moment' and the emergence of a 'post-American world'. Major differences exist between politicians, analysts and journalists regarding the USA's most appropriate route out of its hegemonic supremacy. But it is clear that in a very potent sense the concern over relative decline has shaped US debates about the design of foreign policies.

But where does Europe fit into this picture? While American thinkers and policymakers fret about the big picture, Europe has famously gazed introspectively at its own, very complex institutional navel. During 2010 the EU remained absorbed with putting into place the new institutional structures of the Lisbon treaty. This has streamlined policymaking to some extent, with a newly empowered foreign policy chief in the person of Catherine Ashton, a new European diplomatic service and a modest advance in the integration of the trade and defence sectors. But nearly a year on from the treaty's entry into force, it is clear that these steps have not provided for any qualitative step forward in Europe's international presence.

The EU often appears to be intent on defining its identity

by splitting geostrategic hairs with the USA. It is immersed in laboriously carving out compromises between member-state governments on a seemingly ad hoc basis from issue to issue. Internal agreement between European governments and Brussels-based institutions almost seems to have become an end in itself for EU foreign policy. The EU talks endlessly of its moral sophistication in international affairs. The more it does so, the more it appears blind to the winds of change whipping at the foundations of the global system. Such blasts of transformation tear at the very fabric of the world that gave birth to Europe's model of integration. And yet the EU and its national governments still seem fixated on the idea that this model serves as the basis for Europe's projection into the world.

Only a few years ago, an optimistic strain of thinking prevailed. It was widely asserted that Europe was well prepared to meet the challenges of a reshaped world order. Into the 2000s books were still being written about the EU stepping up to be 'the next superpower'.[2] The European Union was itself seen as an embryonic microcosm of the way that this emerging international system would ultimately function. Europe was synonymous with new forms of power, multilateralism and 'post-national' identities.

Now, a less sanguine view prevails. Europe's international influence is seen as increasingly parlous. Only a decade ago, when the EU appointed its first foreign policy 'high

---

2 Rockwell Schnabel, *The Next Superpower? The Rise of Europe and its Challenge to the United States*, Rowman and Littlefield, Lanham, MD, 2005; Mark Leonard, *Why Europe Will Run the Twenty-first Century*, Public Affairs, New York, NY, 2005; and many others.

representative', in the person of Spaniard Javier Solana, the talk was of the gathering momentum of European global leadership. Now it is of an abiding sense of impotence in international affairs. Europe's future, it seems, is not what it used to be.

This much is now self-evident. Managing decline will be the challenge that conditions all other international policy issues for Europe in future decades. It is time that Europeans began to look more systematically beyond simply reasserting the gloomy trends. How is Europe grappling with its own decline – and how could it be doing so more effectively? How well positioned is Europe to soften the impact of its decline? From its knee-jerk policymaking and institutional complexity, are the outlines of a promising strategy emerging? Or are EU policies heading in the wrong direction? Are the effects of decline an inevitable product of structural global change or in some measure the result of European policy failure? How fundamental a change to European foreign policies is really needed? What should that change be? Is the model of European integration boon or bane: is it the solution to a successful response to relative decline or increasingly a straitjacket? Just how should Europe manage its diluted consequence in international affairs?

The German chancellor, Angela Merkel, phrases the challenge well: the latter half of the twentieth century was about security *in* Europe; the first half of the 21st century will be about achieving security *for* Europe in a reconfigured international order.[3] But how well are European governments repositioning themselves for this needed change of focus?

---

3   *The Times*, 7 January 2010.

The answers to these questions are not comforting. Europe is running in order to stand still. A strange and noxious mix of sullen fatalism and blithe overconfidence envenoms its foreign policies, which are too regressive to benefit from the fact that the emerging international order is replete with positive opportunity, and not only threats. Policies are in need of redirection in five different areas: multilateralism; security; identity; political values; and economics.

Reassessment is needed of the path that European governments have taken in their reaction to imminent decline. Europe cannot turn the clock back. But it can ensure for itself a soft landing in a world beyond Western hegemony. Europe's international role will not be what it was. It will have a less imposing presence in international organisations; it will need to grapple with stiffer competition in foreign investment, trade and even development cooperation; it will need to live with more vulnerability in energy dependence; it will find its core political and social values increasingly questioned; and it will be unable to advance on key future challenges such as climate change without crafting supportive alliances with other powers.

Not all is doom and gloom, however. The growing tendency to paint the future as Europe's dystopia is exaggerated. Erstwhile speculation that Europe was on course to establish itself as the most influential of new superpowers may in hindsight look laughably overblown; but now the tendency is to the other extreme, of thinking that everything quintessential to European approaches in international affairs is in a downward spiral to deserved extinction. Decline in some areas can be combined with new opportunities being seized on other measures. Power should be understood to mean not pre-eminence, but the practical capability to achieve goals. In this sense, the reshaped world order will offer benefits and not merely constraints. Europe can find useful niche roles in international affairs.

A balance is needed: Europe must not stick inflexibly to existing ways of seeing the world, but nor must it drop all core principles in a defensive scramble to adjust to a harsher international system. It must resist the siren call of morose introspection. In many senses the reshaped world order enjoins Europe to revitalise its commitment to what are supposedly core tenets of the EU's international identity, which have ebbed in recent years. If Europe rises to the challenge it can hope to gain much benefit from the post-Western world.

The scale of the challenge

The tide's turn against Western pre-eminence in international politics appears inexorable. Historians remind us that European dominance may be seen in retrospect as but a transient interlude, between a pre-industrial era when Asian powers bestrode many regions of the world and today's re-emergent Far East. The economic statistics are sobering. The European Union's share of world trade will soon dip below 20 per cent. The EU accounted for over a quarter of world GDP in the mid-1990s; it will generate little more than 10 per cent by 2030. Asia's share of world output has doubled from around 15 per cent at the beginning of the 1970s to well over 30 per cent today.

Extrapolations differ in their details, but broadly concur

that within the next three decades China's economy will become larger than that of the entire European Union; that India may not be far behind; and that a further tier of states, such as Indonesia, Mexico, Turkey and South Korea, will catch up to the extent that their voices will hold significantly more weight relative to those of European governments. It is likely that in 2050 no EU country will figure in the world's top ten economies. The 'reflection group' of notables set up to examine the EU's future speculated in 2010 that the shift in economic power was such that the Union risks becoming the 'irrelevant Western peninsula of the Asian continent'.[4]

Emerging powers' multinationals are increasingly over-taking European companies in size, productivity and global reach. Only nine European Union multinationals now appear in the list of the fifty biggest global companies. Asian economies are catching up in research and development expenditure. In addition, Europe's dependency on energy from unstable and non-democratic regions of the world is set to intensify. Some even fear a future of energy wars as the West and rising powers such as China fight for access to a shrinking pool of hydrocarbons. And several Asian economies seem to be stealing a lead in the development of new renewable energy technology.

Moreover, even these prognostics are overly kind to Europe. In comparing 'Europe' with China, Russia, India or Brazil, these statistics are not comparing like with like. They

---

4 Reflection Group on the Future of Europe, 'Project Europe 2030: challenges and opportunities', A Report to the European Council by the Reflection Group on the Future of the EU 2030, Brussels, May 2010, p. 12.

give the EU the benefit of being counted as a single entity alongside individual emerging nations, when it is still to demonstrate that it in fact acts in unified singularity.

The financial crisis has hastened the unfavourable direction of these trends. It leaves Europe's finances more seriously drained just as its pensions crisis assumes alarming proportion. Many experts doubt the sustainability of some fairly core tenets of the European economic model. In Asia the crisis has been one only of aggregate demand, but in Europe it is something more structurally profound. One leading think tank fears 'a distinct possibility that the crisis will be remembered as the occasion when Europe irretrievably lost ground, both economically and politically'.[5]

To the extent that most European states have depended heavily on capital inflows to fund consumption, their model of economic growth will be hit harder than those of emerging markets. Sovereign credit default spreads are now greater for many EU member states than for emerging markets. The financial crisis started in the USA, but now the focus is on trying to save several European economies from meltdown. Far from focusing on reversing decline, the EU has spent much of 2010 in fire-fighting mode, trying to prevent the eurozone from fracturing. The collapse of the Greek economy and the protracted debates over how much Germany was willing to offer to bail southern Europe out of a situation caused by its own profligacy have constituted one of the EU's most profound internal crises; externally they

---

5   André Sapir (ed.), 'Europe's economic priorities 2010–2015. Memos to the new Commission', Bruegel Institute, Brussels, September 2009, p. 6.

have also left the Union's prestige, unity and clout further compromised.

Indeed, it is salutary to record that the financial crisis has triggered International Monetary Fund (IMF) intervention in Europe for the first time in 30 years. The ensuing recession is already eating into European defence budgets. Many predict that Europe's rising debt will emasculate its political power. Many diplomats openly worry that the enormous debt run up in the recovery phase and now the subject of government austerity plans will be the defining feature of Europe's international policies for a generation. Charles Grant laments the fact that just when the Lisbon treaty had finally entered into force the Greek debt and euro crisis has engendered what is likely to be another prolonged bout of introspection.[6] With Britain mired in its own profound economic crisis outside the eurozone, debates in the 2010 UK election campaign were eerily silent on the challenges of international adjustment. The aforementioned reflection group chaired by Felipe González has failed to generate momentum for reform.

As a result of the financial crisis, the G20 has displaced the G8 as the pivotal international economic forum, clearly diluting European influence. One of the most obvious and remarked-upon effects of the crisis is the way in which non-Western powers have assertively sought their overdue place at the top table of international economic governance. Not only has the G20 shifted economic and political power

---

6   Charles Grant, 'Greece rescue is just a sticking plaster', *Guardian*, 30 March 2010.

away from the West, but Europe is now clearly on the back foot in responding to emerging powers' complaints that its broader representation in multilateral bodies continues to be unjustly and disproportionately high. Within the G20, it is striking how Asian economies that emerged from their own financial crisis over a decade ago in robust shape are in no mood to follow strictures on financial regulation from a floundering set of European economies.

Since the 1950s a key source of the EU's international power has been the preferential trade agreement. But this engine has run out of steam. Only a handful of states do not now have preferential access to the EU market: the USA, Australia, New Zealand, Singapore, Japan, Taiwan and Hong Kong.[7] Emerging powers are no longer queuing up to sign trade agreements with Europe – especially when the EU's market-opening offers are invariably stingy and rather 'trade light' – but have rather initiated an enormous number of free trade accords between themselves, cutting out Western powers entirely. If the Doha round of trade talks is eventually concluded, the whole architecture of international trade will change, to the detriment of the EU's traditional commercial mechanisms.

Even in development assistance – for long a key source of European political leverage – the EU now faces competition from new non-Western donors. Europe needs to rethink the role of development aid as a source of influence. Development funds from southern states have risen from

---

7   The EU is now negotiating free trade deals with Canada and South Korea, taking them off this list; Singapore has the prospect of being next.

almost nothing in the 1990s to around 10 per cent of global aid flows.[8] South Korea has recently joined the Development Assistance Committee of leading donors, with a $1 billion annual aid budget. As EU funding becomes tighter and developing states grow, so aid declines as a share of GDP in many poor states. China, India and Brazil are now contributors to the IMF, a long-maligned organisation whose fortunes have recently been revived according to a much less Western-driven agenda.

Politically, the trends appear no more encouraging. The spread of what are often defined as 'Western' values of democracy and human rights has plateaued. Talk abounds of 'authoritarian capitalism' establishing itself as a credible and attractive alternative to liberal democracy. On international security issues, rising powers cooperate among themselves to greater effect. Several of these powers are catching up with Europe in military expenditure and capacity. And not only are non-Western states increasing military expenditure and capability relative to the EU, but violence perpetrated by non-state actors additionally leaves Europeans feeling more insecure. The European ambition to help resolve conflicts in faraway places appears increasingly unattainable. The experiences in Afghanistan and across Africa suggest that the EU has neither the resources nor the political models capable of stabilising violence-prone societies in any sustainable fashion.

---

8   United Nations Economic and Social Council, 'Trends in South–South and triangular development cooperation', Background Study for the Development Cooperation Forum, Ecosoc, New York, April 2008.

For some doomsayers it is demographics which represents Europe's fatal weakness. Robert Samuelson wrote that this more than any other factor portends 'the end of Europe'.[9] The continent will account for under 5 per cent of the global population by 2050, a fall from 12 per cent in 1950.[10] Combining many of these different dimensions, one model arrives at a measure of overall power as a composite of indicators on trade, GDP, population, technology and military expenditure. Under this model, the EU's share of 'global hard power' is predicted to decline from 17 per cent in 2009 to 9 per cent in 2050.[11]

It often appears that, alongside a battery of emerging players, the EU is regarded as a *sub*merging power. Hyperbole should be resisted and a sense of proportion retained. It is not that in objective, absolute terms Europe is enfeebled. But its relative predominance is increasingly compromised. And it is not that, as is often asserted, today's changes are entirely unprecedented in their rapidity. On some indicators the rise of non-Western powers may already be plateauing; the acceleration of rebalancing may at least be slowing. But even though a sense of proportion must be retained, the scale of the challenge is clearly immense.

Then British foreign secretary David Miliband

---

9   Robert Samuelson, 'The end of Europe', *Washington Post*, 15 June 2005.

10 Walter Laqueur, *The Last Days of Europe: Epitaph for an Old Continent*, St Martin's Press, New York, 2007, p. 27.

11 The International Futures Models, available online at www.ifs.du.edu, outlined by Thomas Reinard, 'A BRIC in the world: emerging powers, Europe, and the coming order', *Egmont Papers*, 31, Egmont Institute, Brussels, 2009, p. 25.

summarised: '[T]he choice for Europe is simple. Get our act together and make the EU a leader on the world stage; or become spectators in a G2 world shaped by the USA and China.'[12] For Walter Russell Mead, Europe not only faces the prospect of slightly diminished stature, but stands before the gaping abyss of a whole 'post-European world order' – the end of a global system attuned to European values and interests.[13] With an aphorism that subsequently stuck, in 1962 Dean Acheson cruelly jibed that the UK had 'lost an empire and not yet found a role'.[14] Today we might say something similar of the EU, which appears to have lost its founding imperative, but not settled on its role in a new era of international politics.

Myopic drift
The way that Europe is beginning to deal with these challenges is misplaced and disquieting. As the many fierce currents converge, signs emerge of an inward-looking European defensiveness. As Europe dwindles in stature, so inertia suffocates its international action. Europe stands both overly meek and unduly self-critical of its own drift in policy. It exhibits a curious mix of supine defeatism and stubborn resistance to rethinking.

---

12 David Miliband, 'Strong Britain in a strong Europe', speech at the International Institute for Strategic Studies, London, 26 October 2009.

13 Walter Russell Mead, 'The European world order', *American Interest Online*, available at http://blogs.the-american-interest.com, posted 21 January 2010.

14 Dean Acheson, speech at West Point, USA, December 1962.

The Lisbon treaty was designed to simplify EU decision-making to facilitate a more effective response to the challenge of decline. Nearly a year on from the treaty's entry into force the jury is still out on whether this will prove to be the case. Hope abounds that the new External Action Service (EAS) – the world's biggest diplomatic outfit – will begin to make its mark. Conversely, much initial commentary focused, somewhat viciously, on Baroness Ashton's supposed lack of stature for the job of foreign policy high representative. Spain's most perceptive and erudite senior diplomat, Fidel Sendagorta, sees the low-key appointments of Ashton and Council president Herman van Rompuy, along with the promulgation of only minor procedural changes, to be in tune with Europe's lowered aim of: 'A European Greater Switzerland ... downgrading our ambitions and using our scarce energies to navigate our decline as safely as possible.'[15]

It is certainly the case that the treaty opened another round of internal institutional fine-tuning. The details of the EU's new foreign policy machinery were left highly uncertain by the new treaty, and the fact that their resolution dominated proceedings in Brussels in 2010 again distracted from the big substantive debates hanging unresolved over this ostensibly new beginning for Europe's international presence. Insiders admit that meetings in Brussels have been predominantly devoted to the staffing questions of the EAS, leaving little time for more geopolitical discussion. As Swedish foreign

15 Fidel Sendagorta, 'The Baroness and the haiku writer', BlogEuropa. eu, available at http://blogeuropa.eu/category/fidel-sendagorta/, posted 23 November 2009.

minister Carl Bildt has put it: Europe has been thinking about its hardware, but what good is new hardware if it does not come with updated software?[16]

And in terms of the substantive dimension, the trends are not encouraging. European governments are widely counselled to ditch the erstwhile ethics of their international projection. A typical example of the advice now raining in on European governments asserts that Europe 'must accept a significantly less open economic model, and impose fewer normative demands on non-Western countries', accepting that values can no longer spearhead its influence over international trends.[17] *The Economist* opines that Europe's focus on the values of postmodern peace-building has been a 'holiday from history' that must now end.[18] An epiphany of resurrected realpolitik beguiles European governments.

None of which should surprise us. The tendency evident throughout history has been for crisis and apparent decline – whether in the shape of economic turmoil, rising rival powers or war – to push governments away from all types of liberalism. One of Karl Popper's seminal contributions was to note that crisis encourages governments to seek control and top-down solutions. It makes individuals prone to the appeal of illiberal dogma as a solution to personal anomie. Noting this historical pattern beginning to repeat itself, one

---

16 Carl Bildt, speech at the Annual Conference of the European Union Institute for Security Studies, Paris, 23 November 2009.

17 Franz-Paul van der Putten, 'Time for Europe to take a long, hard look at its global decline', *Europe's World*, Summer 2009.

18 *The Economist*, 31 October 2009, p. 42.

writer concludes, 'The liberal phase in our history seems to be coming to an end.'[19]

The EU has slipped into a mindset that is wistful and obdurate in equal measure. The difficulty of capturing the essence of EU foreign policy is that two things are happening simultaneously. At a strategic level, the EU is increasingly seduced by realist tenets of strategic competition and balancing. At a more technical level the EU's faith in the exportability of its own institutional forms remains unabated. It is this mix which results in the paradoxical combination of exaggeration and immobilism in European strategic planning.

Neither strand of policy response weathers scrutiny. On the one hand, realist misanthropy must be resisted. Liberal apostasy is not the answer to relative decline. In its very name, 'realism' claims a virtue that it in fact fails to demonstrate. It is incongruent with the ever-deepening global interdependence of political and economic life. European foreign policies do indeed need magnanimity and pragmatism, but to principled ends.

On the other hand, Europe must cease to think in terms of those principles being a matter of exporting the EU's own rules, models and identities. While confronting the challenge of relative decline requires robust European unity, mapping a forward-looking and enlightened response also obliges the EU to display a less self-obsessed mode of thinking. Herman van Rompuy has admitted as much, warning that 'Europe

---

19 Ben Wilson, *What Price Liberty? How Freedom Was Won and Is Being Lost*, Faber and Faber, London, 2009, p. 417.

can no longer shine by the force of its example only'.[20]

Too much analytical attention has focused on exactly what type of actor the EU is, how we can best describe its 'actorness' in international relations, whether it exerts 'power' in any traditional sense, and whether it qualifies as a purely or predominantly 'civilian power'. All this terminology-fiddling has masked the gathering clouds of decline. It feeds European obscurantism.

The EU is a complex political system, but it is easy to get dragged into fruitless debate over arcane questions of internal 'competencies', over the question of which institutions have which degree of power within the EU's *sui generis* system of decision-making. To presume that this is the most important issue of analysis overstates the degree to which external policy is a function of internal institutional structures – something that it is now highly fashionable for theorists of European integration to argue. It has led to an implicit assumption that the more integrated at the EU level a particular policy field is, the more effective is the influence that Europe as a whole is likely to wield globally. This is far too simplistic a view. To note this is in no way Eurosceptic, but simply highlights the need for more creative thinking outside the kind of reasoning for so long taken as axiomatic within EU circles.

It is this self-referentialism which leads to the assumption that all the EU needs to do to maximise and retain influence is to continue seeking to disseminate its own model and

---

20 Herman van Rompuy, 'The challenges for Europe in a changing world', address to the College of Europe, Bruges, 25 February 2010.

rules. It is striking how frequently European Union policy-makers insist confidently that, in the words of one interlocutor, by 'drowning the world in EU rules ... we bureaucratise away centuries of conflict'. The EU might not have the formal state-like or hard power of the USA, this line runs, but it enjoys a more effective de facto influence. The assumption is that exporting even very technical rules brings 'a spirit of transparency, the law and compromise'. Again, such thinking looks increasingly lazy and overly optimistic. Many examples exist of countries that adopt EU rules and standards but then go off in an adverse direction in terms of their geostrategic identities. The EU has been seriously dilatory in seeing the power of its own intrinsic institutional nature as infallible.

In sum, an uneasy mix of dynamics conditions current European foreign policy. At a macro-political level there is a tendency towards overreaction. The drift towards geopolitical zero-sum reasoning risks thinking that the future will be played out on terms set by other powers. At the level of more specific policy sectors, the EU tends to under-reaction in presuming that a normative and institutional influence will continue to flow primarily from its own models and structures of cooperation. This strand of European policy looks increasingly heavy, bureaucratic and staid alongside the 'flatter' and less hierarchical institutional forms that prevail in the reshaped world order.

Cutting across these different dimensions is a common and fundamental error in thinking. Europe – its interests, values, strategies and models – is thought of as a transcendentally *a priori* category that hermetically gestates in contradistinction to the 'outside world'. Robert Cooper captured this mode of thinking in counterpoising a postmodern European Union against the 'law of the jungle' beyond EU borders.[21] An elegant and influential formulation; but now such logic is in danger of being taken a little too far.

Europe should not be mobilised as a monolithic entity, but understood as one layer interwoven at many different levels into the complex tapestry of the emerging non-Western world. Europe is both an independent and a dependent variable in the struggle to deal with decline. As an analytical category it should be seen as one – but only one – connection within the complex, overlapping lattices that make up the modern international system. Europe must be judged by its contribution to social, economic and political universalism. At present, its actions curiously militate *against* the globality of those very values and models that sustain cooperation, harmony and integration within Europe itself.

Mapping a response

Europe can retain real influence in world affairs. As others have frequently argued, to do this European governments must on many key issues learn to speak and act in more effective concert. The coordination of European foreign policy through the European Union remains essential and must be deepened in several spheres. But this is only part of what is needed. A deeper rethink is also required. The EU must recognise that relative decline is irresistible, but not overreact geopolitically. It must not be overly defensive in questioning

---

21 Robert Cooper, *The Breaking of Nations: Order and Chaos in the Twenty-first Century*, Atlantic Books, London, 2003.

the moral principles to which it has often laid claim.

The EU's tone is increasingly one of doubt. European foreign policies display excessive credence in zero-sum defensiveness. But this need not be the case, and indeed is not the best way to deal with the world's shifting power balances. The EU is drifting towards a form of 'Euro-nationalism', simply replacing the nationally centred responses to previous crises by similar reactions coordinated at the European level. This is sold as progressive and forward-looking because it is 'European'. But it is not an adequate answer. It is as if the EU is already preparing its own epitaph as the imperilled bastion of progressive, multilateral, postmodern international politics. This mode of thinking must be shaken off, quickly.

If it is to prosper in a polycentric world order, European foreign policy must seek renewal, not lumber on in its current benighted entropy. This should categorically not entail the vainglorious proselytising of 'European values'. The EU should desist from its still-frequent claims that it constitutes some distinctive and exceptional essence of normative power. The challenge is how the EU can become less Eurocentric, while bolstering its defence of essential liberal values. It must not give up on the latter but cease to see their spread through the prism of its own models and rules. This is how the European Union can, in Kalypso Nicolaidis's words, move from seeing itself as an exceptional power to acting as a universal power.[22]

---

22 Kalypso Nicolaidis, presentation to the conference 'How to strengthen the EU as a global partner under the Spanish EU presidency', organised by FRIDE and the Bertelsmann Stiftung, Madrid, 6 November 2009. Also, Kalypso Nicolaidis and Rachel

Jürgen Habermas has famously advocated a European 'constitutional patriotism' as a way of preserving what are held to be the distinctive forms of European social existence. But it is clear that such European patriotism as is emerging is unlikely to be any more tolerant, outward-looking or adaptable than its national variants. Indeed, efforts in this direction already portend a kind of post-national nationalism. This is not the solution for a more cosmopolitan Europe. A far more propitious way forward would be to heed Isaiah Berlin's observation that the whole project of European unity arose out of the demise of totalitarian grand schemes and self-immolating romanticism that enticed Europe back to the liberal values of 'the old universal standards'.[23]

The EU can no longer rely on the serendipity of circumstance and historical legacy. It needs more nimbly to digest international changes to lessen its dyspeptic unease. Of course, in some ways Europe is better positioned than in previous shifts of the world's political tectonics. The generation-shattering violence of previous eras within Europe is unthinkable today. Europe is not imploding. Its decline is that of the swirling torrent flowing into the becalmed and meandering lowland river. The day-to-day impact is only now becoming tangible due to the economic recession and the financial crisis. In some ways it is this very gradualness of decline which militates against the fashioning of

---

Kleinfeld, 'Can a post-colonial power export the rule of law? Elements of a general framework', in Gianluigi Palombella and Neil Walker (eds), *Relocating the Rule of Law*, Hart, Oxford, 2008.

23 Isaiah Berlin, *The Crooked Timber of Humanity: Chapters in the History of Ideas*, John Murray, London, 1990, p. 205.

new responses and breeds such lugubrious fatalism. Very gradual decline can almost be more pernicious; the EU runs the risk of ending up like the proverbial frog sitting passively awaiting his doom in very slowly boiling water. Yet this situation also means that today's Europe can steel itself to take the more enlightened and progressive, less-travelled road out of relative decline.

Some fundamental changes are required, however. So much in Europe's worldview still emanates – even if at a subconscious level – from the horrors the continent suffered during the first half of the twentieth century. Europeans should never forget the values and principles that succeeded in transcending the now unimaginable brutality of that period. These will and must continue to underpin European unity. But in its strategic mindset, Europe must now lower the curtain on this formative period in history. At the most existential level, it must be another set of priorities which today guides Europe's view of the world.

A change of direction in five areas of European international policies is needed:

1. Europe must help usher in less hierarchical forms of multilateralism, qualitatively different to its current old-school approach to the crafting of international alliances.
2. Europe must reverse its slide back into the geostrategic thinking of yesteryear and use its niche in the maintenance of international security to keep alive more holistic and comprehensive solutions to global instability and uncertainty.

3. Europe must rethink its preoccupation with fashioning a 'European identity' on exclusivist terms, which is a forlorn strategy for holding at bay the illiberal and radical ideas that menace the EU both internally and externally.
4. Europe must realise that pulling back from supporting liberal political values globally is not a strategy that is more 'in tune' with the times.
5. And Europe should recognise that trying to create a self-contained and self-glorifying economic identity is not a promising way of dealing with decline.

These aims can be encapsulated in a series of guiding principles for future European foreign policy. The five guidelines suggested here are: to spend less time obsessing about institutional structures; to move beyond the tendency to equate external influence with the export of the rules and regulations of internal EU integration; to think of coordination between EU member states in a far more flexible and multifaceted way; to renew a commitment to universalism, in a way that re-energises support for ethical values; and to think of values as strategic.

In the new international relations, degree of influence can and will be decoupled from structural measures of power. This is where Europe must focus. Its own narratives of the world are increasingly challenged. In response, they must be adapted, modernised, universalised. If they are, this is ground on which Europe can compete in the future. Yet where Europe needs a clarion call for the 21st century, it has politicians either playing to the gallery of politically correct anti-Americanism or mimicking the language of nineteenth-century zero-sum strategic balancing.

Writing 65 years ago, Bertrand Russell was able to predict the long-term changes afoot. And he was able to relate these to a warning from the last time Europe lost pre-eminence: when it slipped into the parochialism of the Dark Ages and for several centuries Arab and Asian civilisations became 'inheritors of the Greek tradition'.[24]

If Europe continues to trade in the currency of resignation it will merely guarantee its own evisceration. The Union is wrong to abjure its liberal identity. Its flight from liberalism is self-defeating. Europe must – and can – bestir itself anew to reverse these trends. If it does so, the EU can retain elements of effective influence as other powers rise. If the EU can be more anticipatory, relative decline may be accompanied by absolute gains in prosperity, freedom and security.

---

24 Russell, op. cit., p. 268.

2
The scramble for new alliances

One thing everyone seems agreed on is that the reshaped world order will require Europe to seek out deeper, firmer and wider-ranging international alliances. It might be cautioned that the contours of the emerging world order are still taking shape. It is too early to be certain what the overarching structural dynamic of this order will be. Even if it is premature to talk definitively of an order with a uniquely multipolar logic, however, it is clear that at least one dimension of the nascent global system will be a more even dispersal of power. Dealing with future challenges will require more inclusive international coalitions. Attention will turn to the conditions under which such alliances are sought.

For the EU this challenge would seem to represent an already well-trodden path. It is widely known that the European Union is strongly committed to multilateralism. It has the lifeblood of shared power and partnership coursing through its veins. But simply repeating the faith in 'effective multilateralism' has become more of a mantra than a comprehensive strategy for managing change. The question is what type of multilateralism is best suited to dealing with international change. On this score, recent trends in EU policies do not augur well.

The temptation is to cope with the growing uncertainty of decline by favouring a state-centred form of multilateralism. Ad hoc and narrowly defined alliances are increasingly favoured. Many new strategic partnerships have been developed on a one-by-one basis with non-European powers, outside multilateral bodies. European governments seem intent on backing a rejigged concert of great powers – with the EU as one such power, battling for its interests against leading regional powers from around the world. Support for multilateral forums is becoming strikingly more instrumental.

A better approach would be for Europe to support a more qualitative reform of multilateral forums. Notwithstanding its rhetoric, in practice the EU's commitment to such a goal has waned. Negotiating a patchwork of strategic partnerships around the world seems a comforting way to regain geopolitical control. But the reassurance is illusory, and the quid pro quos offered increasingly expensive. Europe needs to rediscover the courage of its multilateral conviction.

Multilateral revisionism

Ask any European diplomat to define the keystone to an effective response to relative decline and the response is likely to refer to multilateralism. Multilateral bodies must, it is averred, be used to their maximum as a means of crafting new alliances and cajoling other powers into helping manage global problems. Of course, in many senses Europe can take genuine credit for being the good multilateral. But there are also important shortcomings in its current approach to the reshaping of international politics.

In many respects the EU's multilateralism is backward-looking and self-centred. Multilateralism is, of course, not synonymous with idealism and quite properly encapsulates the measured pursuit of self-interest. But the EU has drifted too far towards conceiving the multilateral as a mere vassal to reconstituted power politics. For the EU ritually to proclaim its multilateralism devoid of power politics is vapid asininity. The EU limits itself reluctantly to accepting a minor diminution of its own historical preponderance in multilateral bodies, but contemplates insufficient qualitative change beyond revamped voting weights and seat alloca-tions. In multilateral bodies Europe is more irredentist than catalyst. The EU's multilateralism is bromide to its own stra-tegic discomfort, not the potion of global rejuvenation.

Retaining power is still seen as synonymous with retaining seats, voting shares and top jobs in international institutions. European governments fight tooth and nail on these questions. Degree of presence is all. A striking example often used is that until May 2010 the Benelux states still had a greater voting share in the IMF than China. In 2009 European governments agreed, under much pressure, to transfer 5 per cent of their voting shares in the IMF to emerging powers; well short of a significant and propor-tionate rebalancing. As European states become borrowers from the IFIs, their over-representation in these same bodies unsurprisingly engenders even greater antipathy. China was reluctant to help with IMF bailouts in part because of its limited representation in the body. Debates in Brussels show

how apparently traumatised the EU was by its 'not being in the room' in the final phase of negotiations at the Copenhagen climate change summit in December 2009.

This is a damaging and counterproductive way to think about future influence. Europe would win greater goodwill and credence by accepting slimmed-down representation in international bodies. This would be of much more benefit that its loss of formal voting weights – in bodies that tend to search for agreement and avoid divisive votes anyway.[1] The Commission makes much of having tripled its staff at the UN in the last two years. This again reflects the tendency to over-prioritise quantitative measurements of presence. New powers have been drawn up during the summer of 2010 to give the president of the Council the same powers as national leaders to speak in UN debates. Such measures may be useful, but are not in themselves the advance they are presented as being.

The endless citing of the Copenhagen summit as emblem of European irrelevance is a diversion: if the EU was marginalised on this occasion it was chiefly because the USA and China both rejected the kind of binding emissions targets to which European states had already committed, not because they excluded the EU from some qualitatively new breakthrough in dealing with climate change. There are problems with the EU's climate diplomacy – see below – but 'being shut out of the room' at Copenhagen is not prime among

---

1 Jennifer Hillman, 'Saving multilateralism: renovating the house of global governance for the 21st century', Brussels Forum Paper Series, German Marshall Fund of the United States, Washington, DC, March 2010, p. 34.

them. Indeed, there was some advantage in the EU keeping clear of the China–USA rearguard blocking actions at the summit.

European governments slip too easily into self-righteous homilies on Europe's superiority as a redoubt of cooperative security. In fact, European powers have been as mercurial in their alliance-building as any supposedly less principled power. Much European action in international bodies is subversive of multilateralism's key tenets of reciprocity and equanimity. It has always been simplistic to suppose that the exercise of power and support for international rules are mutually exclusive strategies. But much European strategy now tilts more towards instrumentality rather than rule-governed constriction of power.

The EU has refused to contemplate reforms to voting in the World Trade Organisation (WTO) that would unlock trade liberalisation, as these would involve diluting its own veto powers. Developing states complain that the EU has sought simply to smuggle more and more issues into the WTO in an attempt to give itself sharper tools for leverage over poorer states, when the basic problem remains the same, namely Western reluctance to open markets to developing nations. In their determination to maintain and upgrade their nuclear deterrence capability, Britain and France have at least skirted the outer limits of the multilateral Non-Proliferation Treaty (NPT). Britain and France both supported the bilateral US–India nuclear deal outside the framework of the NPT.

The EU might decry the USA's instrumental approach to international institutions, but its own record is far from exemplary. European governments appear drawn increasingly to ad hoc 'minilateralism'. Minilateralism refers to cooperative frameworks grouping small numbers of states in a way that extends beyond merely ephemeral alliances. The risk is that this may actually undermine the very multilateral principles that the same governments insist are essential to self-preservation. Many experts actually advocate such minilateralism. But where overly expedient, this favours an informal over an institutionalised multilateralism – and risks denuding the latter of its core appeal.

Parag Khanna's influential book on 'the second world' posits a vision of world politics that captures much of this. It argues that the USA, China and EU now rule as the world's 'natural empires'. These three superpowers are seen as constructing a power base through alliances within their own respective regions, while also competing against each other for alignments with a growing number of 'second world' states.[2] Even if it is not actually very convincing to reduce the structure of world politics to the dominance of a US–EU–Chinese triumvirate, the picture of these three powers pursuing a complex mix of intra- and inter-regional balancing is highly germane.

The EU's own regional initiatives coexist uneasily with multilateral strategies. The EU has gradually taken troops away from UN missions to its own. There are, of course, cases of excellent cooperation between EU missions and the UN; operations in Lebanon and Chad are examples of this. But tensions have also been evident. Recently in

---

2   Parag Khanna, *The Second World: How Emerging Powers Are Redefining Global Competition in the Twenty-first Century*, Random House, New York, 2009.

Somalia and the Democratic Republic of Congo the EU rejected UN calls for troops. Only around 7 per cent of troops deployed under UN peacekeeping missions today come from European countries, a significant reduction in recent years.[3] Developing states complain bitterly that they are expected to provide today's 'cannon fodder', while rich nations parade their multilateral credentials on the basis of risk-free cheque-signing.

The rest of the world sees the EU approaching multilateralism in an increasingly instrumental fashion: as a means to legitimise European involvement in the affairs of weaker states, but certainly not to sanction the involvement of rising powers in European affairs. European diplomats commonly say today that managing decline is essentially about convincing other regional powers 'to do our work for us'. But how does Europe expect them to do so? What are the incentives? Isn't there a hint of neo-imperialism under this cloak of ostensibly progressive multilateralism?

Talks with any emerging-power diplomat soon reveal the perception that, in hanging on to its over-representation, the EU as a whole is today often an obstacle to, not a purveyor of, effective multilateralism. In private conversation, one is taken aback by just how caustic emerging-power diplomats are about Europe's understanding of multilateralism. To some degree, developing nations have already lost patience and moved to create their own rival regional arrangements in trade, security and development. The EU seems to be

---

3   Richard Gowan, 'The EU should do more to support UN peacekeeping in Africa', *CER Bulletin*, 66, Centre for European Reform, London, June/July 2009.

courting many 'second world' powers more than they are courting it.

Ngaire Woods sums all this up astutely: 'We may not be witnessing the dawn of a new era of multilateralism [but] the last gasp of an old-fashioned concert of the great powers.'[4] In Ulrich Beck's well-established terms: regressive prevails over progressive multilateralism.[5]

European governments appear driven by an ad hoc immediacy that is devoid of long-term vision. Mulling on the changing world order and the new vanguard of USA–China relations, Phillip Stephens laments: 'Missing is anything resembling a European view of the shape of things to come.'[6]

The Chinese complain that they do not want a G2 to be the overriding international forum, but the EU has no strategic vision to lead it towards a G3. Respected Indian experts judge that the EU 'has been unable to articulate what role it sees for India in the emerging security architecture.'[7] The EU has a vague faith in the merits of a world of regional blocs. But in practice most diplomacy is not predicated on inter-regional relations but around poles represented by big single states. A constant complaint from the developing world is that the EU's 'big player diplomacy' actually cuts across efforts to tie the largest rising powers into regional cooperation schemes. Moreover, the fact that other regions may be integrating partly in emulation of the EU is not necessarily a source of

---

4   *Financial Times*, 1 December 2009.
5   Ulrich Beck, *Cosmopolitan Vision*, Polity Press, Cambridge, 2006.
6   *Financial Times*, 25 September 2009, p. 13.
7   Harsh V. Pant, 'When will the EU get serious about India?', *Wall Street Journal*, 12 November 2009.

effective European influence, as it is often presumed to be. Indeed, quite the reverse may be true: region-to-region links are increasingly cutting out the Union.

The EU has signed strategic partnerships with Brazil, Canada, China, India, Japan, Mexico, Russia, South Africa, the USA, the African Union and NATO. But most of these have little geopolitical content. Their very proliferation debases their import in the eyes of partners. An EU–India Security Dialogue that began in 2006 has produced little, certainly compared to India's comparable initiative with the USA. The efforts of the new British government in the summer of 2010 to launch a UK–India special partnership similarly focused on investment deals and did not appear to lock into any broader European political strategy towards India. A common African view of the Africa–EU partnership created in 2007 is that this offers funding for a few useful projects, but not the kind of geostrategic framework within which China pursues its policies on the continent.

This is not to suggest that engagement in developing countries or with rising economies should be based on the Chinese model of diplomacy – far from it. But some degree of strategic depth is required in the way that the EU thinks about these relations. Leading security analyst Jolyon Howarth is spot on in observing that no strategic concept guides the current amassing of bilateral 'strategic partnerships'.[8]

While EU–China relations are now deep, embracing

---

8 Jolyon Howarth, 'ESDP in 2020: the need for a strategic European approach', *ESDP@10*, special issue of ESDP newsletter, October 2009, p. 36.

nearly sixty sectoral dialogues, ministers and Commission officials recognise that they are not strategic. The 'strategic dialogue' begun in 2005 is, in the judgement of a recent House of Lords report, a misnomer. Only the UK and Germany have national China strategies.[9] The trade aspects of talks aimed at a new EU–China accord are not progressing, and are holding up political cooperation. Security issues were discussed systematically for the first time at an EU–China summit in 2009; but still with little concrete follow-up.

Moreover, the EU has failed to use its plethora of new strategic partnerships as an instrument for, or a stepping stone towards, deeper multilateralism. Indeed, these appear to be fashioned as a short-term expedient substitute for the latter. Insofar as some strategic logic is evident it is one of improvised and defensive bilateralism. In particular, the EU is trying to focus on a second tier of rising powers such as South Korea, Mexico and Saudi Arabia: a clearer case of the counterbalancing logic could not be imagined, as such alliances are engineered to offset the most powerful emerging powers. Some experts accuse the EU of still having done too little to construct such alliances aimed at counterbalancing Chinese global power.[10] But all this veers towards archaic realism. A key challenge as yet unaddressed is to encourage emerging democracies to progress from being 'recipients' of development aid to taking on responsibilities

9 House of Lords, European Union Committee, 'Stars and dragons: the EU and China', 7th Report of Session 2009–10, House of Lords, London, March 2010, pp. 27–9.

10 François Godement, 'A global China policy', ECFR policy brief, June 2010.

as drivers of democratic change within their respective regions. Conversely, the EU has invested negligible effort in deepening strategic partnership with Japan or in using the latter's support for multilateralism as a primary access point for influencing Asian security dynamics.

Nor does the EU appear to have a coherent, well-worked vision of where transatlantic cooperation fits into the management of Western decline. The Obama presidency is treating the EU as an already declined power, ironically much more than the Bush administration did. The EU has struggled to respond, other than in reactive and ad hoc mode. The USA seems to be working to at least some degree of overarching vision much more than European powers. Transatlantic relations still need to move beyond the standard range of bilateral US–EU concerns to a new 'transatlantic globalism' – the USA and the EU cooperating on broader global challenges.

For too long the EU position consisted of pressing the USA to stick or return to the multilateral path. Now the Obama administration has done this, but is still often challenged by Brazil, India, China and Russia – as these states mix cooperation and confrontation in their 'soft balancing' of the USA. This exposes the insufficiency of Europe passively riding on the coat-tails of a US commitment to multilateralism, and offering no more than platitudinous backing for Washington. The tone has dramatically changed insofar as Chiracian active delight in US decline has mostly disappeared from the European political scene. But still there is little sign so far of the EU seeking to help the USA more smoothly manage *its* decline – an adaptation that will be one of the most important determinants of the reshaped world order.

It is certainly the case that the language of transatlantic globalism has taken root. Herman van Rompuy eloquently suggests that today's 'common story' uniting the USA and Europe is that of partnership in dealing with the new world order and its sobering challenges.[11] The USA now insists that transatlantic cooperation should no longer be centred on security within Europe itself but on the EU and the USA working together to tackle global issues. But members of the Obama administration complain that European governments are resisting such a refocusing. European states, lament US officials, are still thinking of what NATO can do for them more than what they can do for NATO. Many diplomats now talk of the importance of the EU and the USA working together to persuade China to adhere to multilateral rules and norms. But in practice most action of most member states is clearly aimed at undercutting US influence in China to Europe's advantage. And this cuts both ways: Ana Palacio astutely argues that, instead of transatlantic bonds forging an alliance against common decline, Obama's USA has regained normative appeal to some extent at Europe's expense.[12]

In ten years' time the USA will not be able to set the terms of international affairs through hard-power preponderance. The EU will no longer be able to ride on the US coat-tails quite so sanguinely. It needs a deeper, more rules-based order to prepare for this. Ivan Krastev worries that Europeans have

---

11 Herman van Rompuy, 'Transatlantic responses to global insecurity', dinner remarks at the Brussels Forum of the German Marshall Fund, Brussels, 26 March 2010.

12 Ana Palacio, 'Decision time', *The American Interest*, July/August 2010.

still not woken up to the fact that, up to now, the EU has been able to be what it is thanks only to American hegemony.[13]

The structure of international relations is changing so much that the EU needs to move beyond a primary focus on its bilateral relations with a range of individual states. The hub-and-spokes structure of the international system – developing and emerging states having their strongest relations with the West rather than with each other – is giving way to a more dispersed set of relations. The EU's concept of international cooperation has not yet broadened out to take this on board.

The G20 delusion

One of the most important changes in recent years has been the rise of the G20. It is a rise that reveals much of what is blinkered in Europe's approach to the reshaping of the world order. European Union members of the G20 – Germany, France, the UK, Italy, the European Commission, along with Spain and the Netherlands as invited guests – have played a significant role in transforming the G20 from a forum created to monitor the technical aspects of financial regulation after the Asian crisis of 1997 into a prime geostrategic institution. The G20 played a crucial part in stemming the worst of the financial crisis in late 2008 and early 2009, before then spurring recovery measures and commitments to stiffen regulatory oversight of international banking. On the back of this vital economic role, the G20 has begun tentatively to extend its purview to a range of more political issues,

---

13   Ivan Krastev, 'A retired power', *The American Interest*, July/August 2010.

development challenges and climate change. It is held up by many in Europe as the rising star of a new multilateralism.

The G20's rise reflects a curious mix of geopolitical reasoning. European governments have been keen on a forum within which they are over-represented, while several emerging powers see the G20 as a means of making practical progress in circumvention of European preponderance in UN bodies. European support for the G20 constitutes a new search for beneficial alliances. Russia and the EU, for instance, have particularly strong grounds for a new alliance, as both struggle with hastened decline after the financial crisis. In January 2010 Nicolas Sarkozy made a much-reported speech at the World Economic Forum in which he supported the G20 as 'the harbinger of global governance in the 21st century'.[14]

The G20's legitimacy relative to broader multilateral bodies is questionable. It was hardly a roaring success in flagging up the need for stronger financial regulation in time to prevent the crisis. Its membership is clearly arbitrary. Its proceedings are not distinguished by their transparency. Non-state actors get little look-in. Indeed, from the civil society perspective the G20 is a huge step back after long campaigns had begun to succeed in prising open the mainstream international financial institutions to a degree of regularised, non-state participation. Much of the funding the G20 agreed to inject into the world economy through the IMF has gone to states in the EU's own borderlands. Unsurprisingly for a body including the likes of China, Saudi Arabia and Russia, the

---

14 Nicolas Sarkozy, speech at the 40th World Economic Forum, Davos, Switzerland, 27 January 2010.

G20 tramples over broader multilateral efforts in the field of human rights and good governance.

Interestingly, European and especially French support for a politicisation of the G20 mirrors the trend towards 'economic government' within the EU itself: the notion of heads of government meeting to hatch deals and negotiate trade-offs across a broader range of issues, and not only more firmly rules-based international governance. Indeed, Nicolas Sarkozy pushed for an even narrower G14, excluding second-tier emerging powers in a model even more redolent of a great-powers concert.

More than a little populism has coloured the G20's output. France in particular, but also other European members, have focused effectively on the issue of bankers' pay, while the G20 as a whole has disregarded its own commitment to get pre-existing multilateral trade talks back on track – despite the trade dossier being far more important for long-term recovery of the global economy. In practice, G20 exhortations have not prevented members of the forum sticking to their own distinctive national economic philosophies.

The G20 states have even taken it upon themselves to task the wider multilateral institutions with particular assignments after each summit. On what grounds of legitimacy the G20 has rehabilitated such a discredited body as the IMF is not clear. This is the tail of self-appointed, ad hoc multilateralism wagging the dog of rules-based, institutionalised multilateralism.

The G8 was always berated as exclusivist; the G20 risks pitting what is simply a slightly expanded band of insiders against the 172 states left outside the grouping. Those excluded from the G20 have reacted with predictable anger. Several UN reports and events have urged a switchback from G20 to G192. Diplomats at the UN complain that European governments in the G20 have undermined the technical bodies at the UN working on issues such as international tax evasion. The G77 have lobbied furiously against European governments in an attempt to stem the shift in attention away from the UN to the G20. After the less-than-harmonious Toronto summit in July 2010, developing states criticised the G20 for essentially doing the G8´s bidding.

Twenty-eight non-G20 states have set up the rival Global Governance Group, under the stewardship of Singapore. It is pushing to improve linkages between the G20 and the UN, and has been critical of the absence of any formal reporting from the G20 to the UN secretary general. Emerging powers are favouring their own regional solutions in reaction to frustration over a lack of far-reaching rebalancing through the G20. Europe's traditional partners among the least developed states have been vocal in their criticism of the G20. One African ambassador laments that the G20 is predicated on 'economic muscle' more than multilateral principle.

The Nordic states have also been bitter, asking why they should be taking cues on international finance from the likes of Spain and Argentina. They complain that bigger member states and the Commission have grabbed at the chance of shoring up their own power through the G20 rather than supporting a fully inclusive, regionally tiered World Economic Council.

Asian diplomats express strong objections to the

European push for heavy new regulations in the G20; having reformed their regulatory structures after the 1997 crisis, they fear new rules aimed at European pathologies shutting them out of desired access to international capital. The G20 has additionally set up new rivalries between Asian insiders and outsiders in a way that risks cutting across the hitherto 'inclusive' model of Asian integration.

European members could agree on the immediate value of the G20 as a source of new credit and leverage over a number of key rising powers whose liquidity and markets would be crucial to Europe's recovery. Despite the obligatory pre-summit consultations, however, they struggle to articulate a common vision for the G20 beyond this imperative of short-term narrow self-interest.

Divisions between European governments exasperate other G20 members. Within the G20, EU member states have on many issues been positioned at opposite ends of a spectrum of opinion, with final positions ending up nearer those of mid-point states such as India and Brazil. Such division renders somewhat fanciful the constant advocacy of a single EU seat. As *The Economist*'s David Rennie ponders: the UK letting France represent the interests of the City of London? Unlikely.[15]

The Lisbon treaty has not streamlined European representation at G20 summits. This European prevalence in the G20 is in foreign eyes even more galling in light of Europe's contribution to triggering the global recession in the first

---

15 'Charlemagne's notebook', *The Economist*, available http://www. economist.com/blogs/charlemagne/, posted 1 April 2010.

place – its positions representing the perverse and over-bearing rigidity of the impecunious.

Transnationalised multilateralism

Approaching multilateral alliance-building in realist fashion is not the best way to guarantee European interests. The EU errs in overestimating the extent to which competitive power-balancing will and should suffocate all other strategic dynamics. Giovanni Grevi's concept of 'interpolarity' suggests that competitive multipolarity is part of the new strategic script, but that this is accompanied by deepening existential interdependence. Reflecting this, models of cooperative security aimed at enhancing shared interests – rather than relative power to the detriment of others – are still, indeed, increasingly necessary.[16] Many authors have laboured to point out the rather obvious fact that geopolitical 'history' has returned. But the history that is in the making is still different from that ruled by standard bygone power politics.

The standard received wisdom that the EU suffers from liberal soft-headedness is open to question. European governments are engaging with renewed fervour in standard balancing behaviour, while neglecting the interdependence part of the equation. Rising powers are drifting into zero-sum competition against each other, rather than acting as a monolithic block against the West. The EU should resist the temptation to respond in kind.

It is pointed out correctly that alliances do not and cannot

---

16 Giovanni Grevi, 'The interpolar world: a new scenario', Occasional Paper 79, European Union Institute for Security Studies, Paris, June 2009.

divide neatly between democracies and non-democracies. Indeed, but the danger is now of going to the other extreme of the EU being overly servile in courting new alliances. As yet the EU has invested little effort or political capital in trying to get emerging powers signed up to basic principles of liberal multilateralism in return for supporting their enhanced status in international bodies. With some emerging powers already moving to create their own surrogate multilaterals, diplomats appear to doubt the EU's ability to hold emerging powers to such standards.[17]

The EU has developed a storyline on 'rising powers' but not on the 'broader changes needed to multilateralism'. What, for example, is the long-run policy impact of the fact that some of the most powerful states in the world will still be relatively poor countries? Brussels officials admit to having given little thought to this question. At the very least it must mean that if Europe does not more generously help rising powers' economic and political development, they are less likely to incur the costs of helping redress key global problems. Yet these kind of linkages between Europe's multilateral diplomacy, on the one hand, and its human rights and development efforts, on the other, are simply not being made.

In referring to European multilateralism, a common sentiment is that, in the words of one EU diplomat: 'we are incapable of being an old power'. Such claims may be ritual, but they are utter nonsense. The problem is in fact that European governments have not moved on to seeking

---

17 Reinard, op. cit., p. 38.

to fashion anything resembling a 'new' form of international institutional architecture.

President of the European Parliament Jerzy Buzek observes that EU member states have failed to make any contribution to 'modernising multilateralism'.[18] European governments are blinkered to anything beyond the debates over which states are represented in which bodies and to which degree. What has all the talk of 'new economic governance' produced? The resurrection of a discredited IMF and the dusting off of a quirky body formed ostensibly to monitor financial regulatory issues (the G20). Hardly the stuff of a brave new world.

Pressure for a decentralisation of power away from purely intergovernmental deliberations within multilateral bodies has evaporated. There is too easy an assumption that in today's multilateral cooperation efficiency trumps legitimacy and accountability. The EU has, even if passively, allowed the Human Rights Council to be sabotaged into ineffectualness, *inter alia* because in the absence of a broad democratisation of power at the UN, it is today the organ in which the 'spoilers' concentrate their discontent.

While Catherine Ashton was widely pilloried for her low-key opening performance in the European Parliament, in this debate she actually made a rather important observation: the world order is in flux not just because power is shifting from West to East but because it also continues to shift away from all governments towards markets and social

---

18 Jerzy Buzek, remarks at the Brussels Forum of the German Marshall Fund, Brussels, 26 March 2010.

actors.[19] Her peers would have done well to reflect upon how the EU should respond in kind, instead of simply bemoaning the more superficial aspects of the new high representative's personal background.

European policymakers exhibit a highly technocratic view of multilateralism, to the detriment of support for spaces in which transnational networks and cosmopolitan civil society can influence decisions. The EU has been reluctant to back a UN role in supporting democratic governance internationally. European powers have not supported efforts to foment a 'global civics' through, for example, social forums charged with ensuring that governments meet their promises to protect citizens around the world from genocide and serious human rights abuses.[20] They have frustrated the kind of civic participation in multilateral bodies that would shine a spotlight on their actions – or inaction.

Experts have been debating the prospect of a 'new multilateralism' for a long time. But this remains work undone. Dozens and dozens of initiatives, forums and proposals have, over the years, pushed for a more participative and multi-actor form of multilateralism. But those at the forefront of this cosmopolitan agenda today despair that such options are 'fading away', receiving progressively less support from Western governments. Civil society involvement in the UN remains 'rudimentary', 'decorative' and bereft of tangible

---

19 European Union, 'Address by HR Catherine Ashton at the joint debate on foreign and security policy', European Parliament Plenary, A34/10, Strasbourg, 10 March 2010.

20 Hakan Altinay, 'The case for global civics', Working Paper 38, Brookings Institution, March 2010, p. 5.

influence. No parliamentary assembly has been established in the UN, even in the various highly curtailed forms suggested over the years. The International Court of Justice is not open to cases brought by citizens rather than states.[21]

. European governments have not supported some of the most widely advocated reforms to the United Nations, involving bringing civil society representatives into UN decision-making, a global tax to fund the United Nations or parliamentary-style scrutiny mechanisms within the body's various thematic institutions.[22] The often-raised idea of creating a WTO ombudsman with greater powers to place citizen interests on the trade agenda has not found widespread favour among governments. Neither have efforts to empower the Organisation for Security and Cooperation in Europe's (OSCE) parliamentary assembly attracted significant backing from the majority of EU member states. Alliance-building on hard security issues has subjugated European promotion of social and economic rights in multilateral bodies.

There has been little willingness to strengthen civic watch-dogs of international financial institutions (IFIs), which might provide a more accurate service than the commer-cially driven credit-rating agencies that performed so disas-trously in the financial crisis. Indeed, the trend is in quite the opposite direction: insiders say that dirigisme in economic responses to the crisis is creeping into broader approaches

---

21 Daniele Archibugi, *The Global Commonwealth of Citizens: Toward Cosmopolitan Democracy*, Princeton University Press, Princeton, NJ, 2008, ch. 6.

22 Commission on Global Governance, *Our Global Neighbourhood*, Oxford University Press, Oxford, 1995.

to multilateralism too. A key finding of a recent high-level project on emerging changes to global economic governance is that current reforms are limited to enhancing executive forms of multilateralism 'characterised by state-generated blueprints premised on a grand design'; more states are at the top table but the process is still driven by financial technocrats.[23]

A recent World Economic Forum report similarly laments that limited attention is being paid to the need to include the whole gamut of non-state actors that today are a key part of global affairs within a more pluri-dimensional multilateralism. The world is changing too fast and revolves around too broad a range of important actors for a managerial form of multilateralism to be tenable over the long term. There has been little support for the systematic incorporation of new technologies and the immense potential these bring for scrutiny. Many may dismiss social network and other technologies as gimmicks, but it is still striking how little space is being given to new means of monitoring opaque international bodies. In health and some environmental issues some non-state stakeholders have been given formal involvement in decision-making. But this is not the case in relation to more political issues. Ideas for according national parliamentarians a greater role have also not prospered.[24]

---

23 Andrew Cooper and Paola Subacchi, 'Overview', in Andrew Cooper and Paola Subacchi (eds), 'Global economic governance in transition', *International Affairs*, 86(3), special edition, May 2010, p. 609.

24 World Economic Forum, 'Everybody's business: strengthening international cooperation in a more interdependent world', WEF, Geneva, 2010, pp. 30 and 144.

Climate change conceit

One area of policy stands out as a vitally important example of these trends. Climate change is an issue that many see as being in the vanguard of Europe's commitment to cooperative problem-solving based on a push for more firmly entrenched multilateral rules. There are many aspects of European climate change policy that lie well beyond the scope of this book; but one which is highly relevant to the EU's future international influence is the extent to which the environmental challenge spawns more effective multilateral cooperation. In this vein, climate change is a microcosm for much that is right but also wrong with European approaches to multilateralism.

The cornerstone of the EU approach has been to lead by example. Progress at the multilateral level can best be assisted by Europe pushing ahead with emissions reductions and being generous in providing money to help poorer states cut pollution. The EU asserts regularly that its own actions light the way towards broader international commitments and rules. This is said to be the spirit of Europe's contribution to a stronger multilateral architecture to guide climate change policies, as it avoids momentum-sapping niggling over the distribution of short-term adaptation costs.

The reality is a little more complex. The EU was a firm supporter of the Kyoto treaty – something which is rightly publicised as one of the most significant symbols of the European commitment to rules-based multilateralism. It was in part at the EU's behest that Kyoto exempted developing nations from emissions reduction targets. The EU's Emissions Trading Scheme (ETS) is the world's most advanced cap-and-trade mechanism for reducing emissions. In January 2008 the EU agreed its '20/20/20 by 2020' plan, under which it commits to reducing greenhouse gas emissions by 20 per cent, obtaining 20 per cent of its energy from renewable sources, and increasing energy efficiency by 20 per cent. In mid-2010 it was announced that the EU was on course to meet its emissions target – albeit thanks in part to the recession having lowered the level of economic output.

Critics suggest, however, that the ETS has been framed so as to avoid firm discipline being imposed on emissions levels. ETS allowances are so generous that the carbon price has remained low. Over 150 – many heavily polluting – economic sectors remain outside the scope of the ETS. Experts say that the ETS has been of insufficient rigour to provide the incentives necessary to bring new breakthrough environmental technologies to the market.[25] Investment in renewables fell in 2008 for the first time in twenty years, and this target does not appear to be on course to being fulfilled.[26] By August 2010 less than half of member states had complied with the commitment to produce plans for renewable energy development; and several states, including France, Germany and Spain, are now slashing support to the renewable sector.[27] Crucially, far from being the seed of

25 Arianna Chechi, Arno Behrens and Christian Egenhofer, 'Long-term energy security risks for Europe: a sector-specific approach', CEPS Working Document 309, Centre for European Policy Studies, Brussels, January 2009, p. 42.

26 Nick Butler, 'Why global energy markets need governing', *CER Bulletin*, Centre for European Reform, London, February/March 2009, p. 2.

27 Platts EU Energy, Issue 238, 30 July 2010, pp. 12–13.

broader multilateral cooperation, the ETS allows European countries to purchase 'cuts' in emissions from third countries through carbon trading. The 20 per cent target refers to European production, not consumption; production can easily be transferred to developing countries, wherein European companies may actually increase emissions further. One highly regarded energy expert describes this as 'sidestepping Europe's responsibilities to the developing world'.[28] This looks suspiciously like classic zero-sum behaviour rather than the enlightened problem-sharing of the genuine multilateralist.

While the EU has certainly been ahead of other powers in laying down formal targets for emission reductions, at the December 2009 Copenhagen summit the EU made the extent to which is was prepared to reduce carbon emissions the subject of tit-for-tat negotiation. It stuck to a 20 per cent unilateral commitment rather than a widely touted 30 per cent cut specifically because other states did not agree binding targets. Asked in March 2010 whether the EU would return to considering a 30 per cent reduction target, Commission president José Manuel Barroso argued, 'there is not a great urgency for this now when you see that in Copenhagen some of our main partners were indeed suggesting that we should do less than what we are doing right now'.[29] When the Commission proposed reviving the 30 per cent commitment in May 2010, a number of member states opposed such an

---

28 Dieter Helm, 'EU climate-change policy – a critique', Smith School of Enterprise and the Environment, University of Oxford, September 2009, p. 9.
29 *Financial Times*, 23 March 2010.

increased effort.[30] As a result, the Commission was forced to drop the proposal. (As this book goes to press, France, the UK and Germany have announced they may just be willing to support a resurrection of the Commission's plans.)

All this may be judged sensible negotiating tactics and hardly makes the EU the villain of the piece. But it compromises the claim to unadulterated, vanguard commitment. The EU undercuts its own argument that strong climate change policies make good economic sense. Now it acts like a patient saying to one equally stricken: I will take my pills only if you take yours too.

Moreover, European states have resisted international rules that would remove their own margin for manoeuvre domestically. While they preach climate change multilateralism, many European governments have adopted measures quite clearly contrary to such an ethos. The EU sanctioned a spate of new coal plants in 2008. In Spain, Prime Minister José Luis Rodríguez Zapatero has refused to remove coal subsidies to meet climate change targets. Indeed, a new Spanish law obliges power utilities to use domestic coal, while a massive increase in aid to the country's coal mines has been forthcoming.

Europe's rhetoric is still not matched by hard-cash contributions to the multilateral funds about which its leaders wax lyrical. European contributions to the UN Adaptation Fund have been minimal, at less than 50 million euros a year. Support for the much-praised Global Climate Change Alliance is actually rather limited. The Commission allocated

---

30 *New Europe*, 16–22 May 2010, p. 17.

this initiative only 60 million euros for 2008–10, while few member states support it with meaningful money.[31]

Nick Mabey has described the scale of climate change financing forthcoming for poor states as 'pitiful'.[32] The World Bank has been scathing about Europe's limited support for multilateral financing initiatives and for turning inwards to prioritise domestic vested interests during the recession. It is not even clear that the modest amounts of money committed will be additional to existing development aid – something for which the EU has suffered particularly strong opprobrium from climate campaigners. An EU–China Partnership on Climate Change has benefited from European Investment Bank loans, but money for a third phase of this partnership focused on carbon capture is now running out. By mid-2010 the EU was already falling behind on even the limited degree of climate change finance promised at Copenhagen. The new Conservative-led UK government has targeted external climate initiatives as one of the prime areas for cutbacks.

Moreover, prior to Copenhagen the offer of such funding was made conditional on developing countries accepting emissions reductions of equal magnitude to rich states, in contravention of previous UN agreements.[33] The EU also

---

31 European Think-Tanks Group, 'New challenges, new beginnings. Next steps in European development cooperation', DIE, ODI, FRIDE and ECDPM, Bonn, London, Madrid and Maastricht, February 2010, p. 27.

32 Nick Mabey, 'Sustainability and foreign policy', in David Held and David Mepham (eds), *Progressive Foreign Policy*, Polity Press, Cambridge, 2007, p. 110.

33 Euractiv.com, 11 September and 22 September 2009; *Financial Times*, 11 September 2009, p. 5.

refuses to relax intellectual property rights so as to enable developing states to build up alternative-source technology, instead protecting their own domestic industries in this field. Nor are new renewable energy strategies entirely devoid of realpolitik. Indeed, the quest for renewable resources risks becoming as strategically rapacious as history's erstwhile scramble for oil.

The link between climate change and the principles guiding other dimensions of alliance-building is also becoming difficult to manage. Many European diplomats are entirely candid in arguing that pressure on human rights and peace-building is and will be forgone in order to get the maximum number of countries signed up to internationally agreed climate change commitments. Indeed, some even argue that democratisation in many developing states would make it harder for regimes to make the concessions necessary to cut emissions.[34]

Crucially, at their summit in March 2010, EU leaders committed themselves to emphasising the G20 as a promising body to make progress on climate change – alongside the UN but also reflecting impatience with the 192-state United Nations Framework Convention on Climate Change (UNFCCC). They expressed impatience with a number of self-declared 'anti-imperialist' states having played grandstanding politics at Copenhagen. Developing countries more broadly immediately criticised this EU move as a pretext for escaping pressure to increase climate funds as a quid pro

---

34 David Shearman and Joseph W. Smith, *The Climate Change Challenge and the Failure of Democracy*, Praeger Publishers, Westport, CT, 2007.

quo for international agreements. They have also expressed concern over the EU's own regional energy initiatives – such as the Energy Community drawing in the Balkans, and being extended to Ukraine, Moldova and Turkey – cutting across a multilateralisation of broader energy policy.

EU strategy appears bereft of any notable enlightened foresight on the long-term security repercussions of climate change. Strategists have begun to reflect on the startling absence of a 'European geostrategy' aimed at thinking through how the EU should be securing access to global trade routes, tempering the dangers of strategic bottlenecks and dealing with climate-security linchpin states around the world.[35] None of the profound changes to global political geography that will occur are anywhere near being integrated into strategic planning.[36] The EU has talked of the importance of addressing the broader security implications of climate change, of the latter being a 'conflict multiplier'. But in practice, its security policies carry on as normal with little multilateral commitment on these vital questions.

Conclusion

The way in which multilateralism is structured is a prior consideration that will condition all other policy areas covered in this book. There are two dimensions of multilateralism that require reform – that is, two dimensions in

---

35 See the excellent blog run on European geostrategy at http://ideasoneurope.eu.

36 Cleo Paskal, 'From constants to variables: how environmental change alters the geopolitical and geo-economic equation', *International Affairs*, 85(6), 2009, pp. 1143–56.

which European governments currently fall short in anticipating future trends. These can be seen as the two dimensions
across which multilateral institutions must be democratised,
one a horizontal and the other a vertical democratisation.

First, rising powers need to be offered more genuine and
proactive ownership of the international institutional architecture. As one Brookings Institution report puts it: Western
governments are still asking rising powers simply 'to dock
into the existing ports of the post-World War II institutional
architecture'.[37] They expect these powers to be passive down-
loaders of multilateral commitments, rather than partners
in redesigning the software of international cooperation.
European governments need to realise that sharing out
power within international bodies will produce better decisions and make it more likely that decisions will be respected
by non-Western states. The longer the West takes to entice
rising powers into firmer multilateral rules, the harder it
will be to achieve this objective: as the balance of power
swings, there may only be a relatively short window of such
opportunity.

Second, the multilateralism of the future must incorporate the more systematic input of civil society, the
business sector and other non-governmental actors. Several
European leaders clearly have a vision of international affairs
being driven much more by elite talks, often replicating the
informal fireside conflabs of yesteryear. So far the vision
is: the great and good by the Aga, rather than a global agora.

---

37 Brookings Institution, Center on International Cooperation and
    NYU Abu Dhabi Institute, 'Emerging powers, global security and the
    Middle East', Meeting summary, Abu Dhabi, 9/10 February 2010, p. 4.

The concept of cosmopolitan democracy was suggested a long time ago as the shape of things to come. But European actions have done as much to delay as to enhance a democratised multilateralism.

A more democratised multilateralism, predicated on a global civic engagement, is likely to be beneficial to longer-term European interests. Opening up the international financial institutions can help get civil society allied with European thinking against more purely realist international powers. It will also move ossified international structures in the direction encouraged by technological change. Interdependence at the social level still deepens apace; despite all the focus on rising powers, this social evolution will be an equally important marker of change in the emerging world order. Such network governance is to be harnessed; seeking to resist it is futile as a strategy for the pursuit of state control. State-centric multilateralism appears in essence little more than containment, albeit dressed in finer-sounding internationalist garb. And history has proved containment to be a shaky basis upon which to rest the calculus of self-interest.

The G20 may ultimately provide a boost to global cooperation. But it has been supported by its European members at least in part as a results-oriented substitute for such broader multilateralism. Such pragmatism is understandable while in crisis management mode, with the financial system wavering on the precipice. Over the longer term, however, reifying the G20 as the pre-eminent steward of global economic governance might not prove entirely benign.

Even in the field of climate change, supposedly the vanguard of European multilateralism, EU member states are playing fast and loose. While they clearly desire multilateral deals on the core principles of addressing climate change, their negotiating strategies are far from being entirely benevolent. Anthony Giddens weighs in against the growing risk of democratic rights being seen as expendable in the pursuit of climate change deals. Opening up civic debate, he asserts, is less a danger to tackling climate change than a necessity to make governments more responsive to citizens' demands for action.[38]

None of this is to be naive in thinking that European governments can or should be anything other than interest-seeking animals. The search for new alliances and strategic balancing forms a perfectly proper and desirable part of Europe's adjustment to the reshaped world order. The question is what kind of values should underpin such alliances, as the best long-term guarantor of strategic governability. Here a mid-point is required between, on the one hand, allying only with pro-Western democracies against other powers and, on the other hand, entirely expedient alliances. The G3 vision is simplistic as a description of contemporary international politics and short sighted as advocated strategy. Power must be understood in its broadest sense, as preserving instrumental alliances but also in terms of seeking to shape identities and agendas.

When analysts predict how certain states are likely to act towards the prevailing structure of an international system, their standard comparison is between status quo and

---

38 Anthony Giddens, *The Politics of Climate Change*, Polity Press, Cambridge, 2009, p. 158.

revisionist powers. But it is not obvious how this division should help us assess the EU's role in relation to the current world order. Would we expect the EU to be a status quo power by virtue of its relative prosperity and stability? Or a revisionist power by virtue of its impending decline and the fact that the system no longer works so overwhelmingly to its advantage? This is more than an academic conundrum: the difficulties in answering this basic question are what lie at the heart of Europe's confused adherence to a 'bounded multilateralism'.

3

Maximising a bit part in security

Many foresee the world's big security issues increasingly being determined by the USA and China, occasionally with Russia also as a key protagonist. To the extent that this is correct, it poses the question of how Europe should play its hand as it settles into a more secondary security role. The European Union has long proclaimed its resistance to the undue militarisation of international affairs. It remains correct to insist that contemporary problems do not lend themselves to military solutions. But the reshaped world order does require some careful rethinking about security. Long gone are the heady days of the early 1990s when optimists dared to believe that hard security capacity was no longer of prime importance in a world headed towards liberal harmony. Europe has failed to keep apace in devising updated security doctrine as the world changes. The EU falls short in both hard and soft areas of security. Its hard power is used too timorously to accord it strategic leverage. Its soft power is wielded in too hesitant a fashion to be curative.

Moreover, despite all its rhetoric, the European Union increasingly over-invests in traditional defensive military capacity and falls short in its efforts to tackle the accumulating threats of the new world order – challenges such as cross-border drug trafficking and crime. A strand of 'zero-sum' thinking is creeping back into European strategising. Furthermore, there is evidence that the EU is now drawn towards new security pacts with the likes of Russia which are based on a 'spheres of influence' logic. These are the sort of antiquated buzzwords of an era of international security that Europe was supposed to have left behind.

European efforts to stem the proliferation of weapons of mass destruction are cast in far too narrow and traditional a mould. Indeed, at present, Europe's lacklustre performance in several dimensions of security is more emblematic of, rather than an antidote to, European decline. To knit different areas of policy together, Europe needs a more forward-looking vision of how its compromised power can deal with and contribute effectively to international security challenges. Europe's enunciation of its strategic identity needs to be less bombastic, more astute.

Stepping back

Experts and diplomats have long alluded to the EU's supposedly unique disposition to shape the values of the world around it as part of its approach to geopolitics. Faced with uncertainty and reduced power, however, the understandable temptation will be to pull up the drawbridge and hunker down behind the ramparts. And governments are already ceding to this temptation. This may be an understandable reaction but it is the wrong way for Europe to manage decline.

Contrary to their rhetoric, European governments appear

increasingly less convinced that domestic security requires significant commitment beyond EU borders to address the complex and myriad sources of turmoil. Many observers and policymakers are concluding that resolving conflict in distant states is now beyond European capability. The peace-building agenda is in crisis. The European contribution to tackling global conflict is certainly being scaled down. The lack of success in Afghanistan has proved especially salutary and has encouraged a constriction of European approaches to building resilient states in unstable parts of the world.

Europe is increasingly anaemic in its commitment to a proactive role in international security. One European minister confides: 'public opinion is pushing us towards isolationist positions'. The Switzerland metaphor is gaining currency and brought up surprisingly often by European policymakers, denoting the notion of the EU abdicating from a proactive and interventionist role in international security. The EU has sold such an avuncular image of itself that its strategic presence now lacks bite. It appears to many that Europe is heading towards superfluity in international security.

The scale of today's security challenges is undoubtedly daunting. They are certainly beyond the reach of a less powerful Europe definitively to 'resolve' on its own. But this sets the bar too high and is the wrong way to conceive the predicament. Europe's incipient retreat back into approaches based on containment is a mistaken, knee-jerk response to decline. Managing decline requires a greater, not lesser, involvement with the international genesis of instability. Despite its loss of relative power, Europe has the capacity to be doing far more to make a productive contribution to lessening the violence and instability that rebound on its own interests.

But what about the Common Security and Defence Policy (CSDP)? With 28 CSDP missions undertaken during the last ten years, many will protest that it is surely nonsense to talk of Europe 'stepping back'. But most CSDP deployments have been so limited in scale as hardly to merit the label of 'missions'. A handful of lawyers sent to an unstable Georgia; a few score police officers arriving in dribs and drabs and without a clear mandate in the vortex of Afghanistan; a rule-of-law mission to Iraq that has four times more people sitting in Brussels than in Iraq; half a dozen security sector specialists dispatched to Guinea after the country's president is killed … all positive, but hardly earth-shattering, world-shaping contributions. The much-lauded but unused 'Battlegroups' that now form the ostensible backbone of the CSDP are so small as to be a distraction. The Lisbon treaty provides for CSDP pioneer groups to unlock deeper security activism; but these are unlikely to have great impact if the mode of intervention continues to be so circumscribed.

Indeed, it is striking that the CSDP has developed more than the strategic dimensions of common EU foreign policy output. The significance of an ad hoc set of missions is emphasised as a substitute for global security policy. If Europe were on the psychologist's couch, CSDP would be diagnosed as displacement activity.

It is invariably the case that while the EU dispatches its modest peace support missions it adopts positions on the high politics of security that undermine those very same deployments. The Union has run a monitoring mission in Georgia since the Russian invasion of the southern Caucasus state in 2008, nominally to help preserve Georgian territorial integrity. But the EU's special representative to the southern Caucasus freely acknowledges that at the same time the EU is seeking ways to engage with and in South Ossetia and Abkhazia – with implications for debates over the status of the two disputed enclaves within Georgia. The EU resumed trade and cooperation talks with Russia despite the latter abrogating the ceasefire deal arrived at through the offices of European leaders in 2008.

The level of ambition for the CSDP remains modest. States such as France have rebuffed Turkey's interest in participating more in the CSDP. This damages what would be a major capacity boost for Europe's security presence and in turn has slowed down EU–NATO rapprochement. A current diplomatic joke runs that European ambivalence in NATO suggests that the acronym stands for 'Not At The Office'. Because of European strategic caution, many observers fret that the EU and NATO are on the road to divorce. Leading a series of consultations among senior politicians, Robin Niblett points to the shared recognition that the UK elections of 2010 will usher in a period of weakened British involvement in international security.[1]

If an absolutely key determinant of the reshaped world order will be the need to help China overcome its insecurity complex, then the complete disengagement of Europe's security strategies from this dilemma must count as a

---

1   *Financial Times*, 28 April 2010, p. 7.

particularly serious oversight. In turn, Association of South-east Asian Nations (ASEAN) diplomats complain that the EU has no overall strategic vision for their region and is offering little to help South-East Asian states deal with the challenges presented by a rising China. A constant complaint is that the EU's only approach seems to be to sell a model of integration that does not coincide with the ASEAN preference for less institutionalised coordination. This is a negative factor in the region rather than a source of positive influence. Leading with a purely trade-based strategy no longer suffices as intra-Asian commerce has rocketed and region-to-region trade talks with the EU are floundering. Without its own equivalent of the US 7th Fleet patrolling Asian waters, the EU cannot be a leading player in Asian security, but diplomats from the region express frustration that European governments have engaged so little even with non-traditional forms of security. Kishore Mahbubani labels Europe's cold-shouldering of Asia in the wake of the latter's late-1990s financial crisis 'one of its stupidest strategic decisions'. (Unfortunately Mahbubani's familiar call for the EU to extol the Asian model of authoritarian development also exhibits just the kind of self-glorifying hubris he despises in Europeans).[2]

Pakistan provides one of the most conspicuous examples of Europe's disinclination to engage meaningfully in security. Despite all its rhetoric about tackling the economic roots of instability, and some increased diplomatic efforts from 2009, the EU has refused to grant Pakistan its standard set of

---

2   Kishore Mahbubani, 'Europe is a geopolitical dwarf', *Financial Times*, 21 May 2008.

(zero-quota) trade preferences. EU development aid to this socially divided and economically blighted crucible of global jihad is pitifully limited. Indeed, in 2010 European humanitarian funding has declined and a number of aid initiatives closed down. Baroness Ashton did not even bother to attend the second EU–Pakistan summit in June 2010. The absence of a comprehensively political European strategy is striking. This despite the well-established analysis that radicalism has been fuelled in Pakistan by a covert alliance of convenience between the venal political elite and the conservative religious establishment.

In Afghanistan EU troop levels have increased to nearly thirty thousand but remain modest relative to the scale of the challenge. And many of those troops that are present operate under restrictive rules of engagement that prevent them from doing much real fighting against the Taliban. Reflecting the impact of these national caveats, US troops sneer that Europeans have mistaken ISAF (the International Security Assistance Force) as standing for 'I Stay Away From Fighting'. Some EU member states have put in a small number of extra troops, but as a gesture to President Obama and as a means of repairing the general transatlantic relationship more than with the intent of assuming joint responsibility with the USA. The USA still expresses despair at European foot-dragging in filling training positions, in coordinating with NATO and in using its police officers effectively in Afghanistan.

The fall of the Dutch government in March 2010, over the refusal of part of the coalition to keep the country's troops in Afghanistan, was only the most dramatic instance of broader

European unease. The inability of the Dutch government to agree on extending its Afghan mission in part reflected domestic political manoeuvring; in part a more isolationist trend; and in part the cost of keeping troops and equipment in Afghanistan during a period of budget cuts. In the UK, the new Cameron government has recommitted troops and increased aid but has also set a 2015 end-point to deployment in Afghanistan.

Nearly eight years on from the invasion that ousted the Saddam regime, the European commitment to stabilising Iraq remains pitifully limited. France and Germany remain reluctant to commit resources. The Commission has channelled funds to Iraq through other multilateral bodies but this support is now being phased out. The Commission barely operates cooperation programmes itself. Even key coalition members such as Denmark and Poland have not only withdrawn soldiers but also downsized aid efforts. Virtually all EU member states are decreasing development aid to Iraq. The UK has committed much to the country in 'blood and treasure'. But the limits to its deployment and mandate led to a humiliating defeat and withdrawal in the south of the country. All this despite frequent pleas from Iraqis for the EU to forget differences over the invasion itself and offer a non-negligible contribution to dealing with the country's formidable security challenges.

Nor has the EU invested significant sums in what analysts refer to as 'non-traditional' security issues. The EU is not well set up to link its external security policies to issues of internal risk. In Latin America the EU has run counter-narcotics programmes for over a decade which formally aim at offering alternative development paths to drug culti-vation. But the amounts offered have been negligible and are easily over-shadowed by the USA's more law-enforce-ment-based approach. Dialogue forums have been run in Andean countries to improve understanding between local communities and state bodies, but with annual funding of only a few tens of million euros these are few in number. The EU has declined to engage with local security forces on capacity-building and reform issues. One Commission official admits that no one in the EU is linking in a compre-hensive way the approach to fragile states with the solutions needed to restrict cross-border crime and illicit trafficking. Narcotics and crime represent increasingly serious problems that impact on European security but which are treated in an extremely modest way.

In sum, increasingly the EU merely dips its toe into the choppy waters of international instability. The EU's concept of security is still Eurocentric as opposed to Eurasian, which is the scale at which most problems occur today. Chris Patten bitingly laments 'Europe's propensity for offering every sort of assistance short of real help'.[3] As Daniel Korski has taunted, the EU is becoming the world's armchair general, issuing advice to all and sundry without putting itself on the line. Alternatively, the EU can be likened to the boy who cried wolf: so many times has it rubbished hard power as anachronistic that when it does see a genuine need for some strategic bite it lacks conviction and credibility.

---

3   Chris Patten, *What Next? Surviving the Twenty-first Century*,
    Penguin, London, 2009, p. 60.

Not quite the pacifist

The best-known and most commonly aired critique of European security policy is, of course, that EU states fail to pull their weight on basic military expenditure. The EU's dearth of hard security power is often posited as the most alarming sign of its global decline. But the shortcomings of European military capacity are more subtle in nature. Redressing decline is not primarily a question of pumping up military budgets. The lack of political commitment to use this capacity in an enlightened milieu-shaping way, as described above, is by far the more constraining trend.

It is somewhat puzzling that the notion that Europe is a kind of pacifist, global hippy has taken such firm root. US Defence Secretary Robert Gates ruffled European feathers in February 2010 when he stated that: 'The demilitarisation of Europe has gone from being a blessing in the 20th century to an impediment to achieving real security and lasting peace in the 21st.' But the thrust of his argument is wrong. Pacifism is not the area of major weakness in European policies.

Trends in military capability are diverse. It is well known that despite relatively high levels of defence expenditure, European states struggle to deploy more than a small percentage of their soldiers to conflict zones. It is true that military expenditure in emerging powers is rising faster than in Europe. In 2009 Asia overtook the EU in defence expenditure. But five EU states still appear in the top fifteen military spenders worldwide.[4] Overall EU defence expenditure has

---

4   Stockholm International Peace Research Institute, 'Trends in military expenditure', SIPRI, Solna, 2008.

risen in absolute terms over the last decade but has fallen as a share of GDP, from just over to just under 2 per cent of national income. In 2009, Italy, Spain and central European states cut overall defence expenditure significantly. In 2010, France, Italy, Germany, Austria and Spain, as well as several central European states, announced further defence cuts. France and Germany are together seeking nearly 15 billion euros of cutbacks up to 2014; in consequence, in summer 2010 they created a new working group to make further efforts to reduce duplication in military procurement. The USA spends six times more on defence research and development than all EU member states combined.

On the other hand, the EU's code of conduct on arms sales has not significantly reduced arms transfers to dictatorial regimes that flagrantly use weaponry to repress their own populations. One of the main sources of tension with the USA in recent years has been the dramatic increase in European arms sales to China and the constant effort by most EU states to remove the arms embargo imposed on the Chinese regime after the Tiananmen Square killings. European arms sales to Nigeria have more than doubled since 2007, just as conflict there has intensified; these sales are now several times the magnitude of European development assistance to the country. BAE Systems is still the second-largest arms exporter in the world. Eight European companies are in the top twenty global arms sellers. In 2010 France agreed to sell a state-of-the-art warship to Russia, to the fury of central European member states.

So, the picture is mixed. European military spending could be higher, but the EU is far from being the purely soft power it is often described as. The bigger problem is the *way* in which European governments spend their defence budgets. European security set-ups are still oriented towards defence against interstate conflict. But this is no longer the most pressing risk.

Security provision remains too oriented towards the big defensive 'platforms' that were ostensibly seen as things of the past. While there has been some reconfiguration away from traditional defensive heavy equipment such as tanks, European inventories of outdated Cold War-oriented equipment remain high.[5] The UK has committed to putting two large new aircraft carriers into operation by 2015 and upgrading its Trident nuclear deterrent. The UK's huge, £20 billion investment in updating Trident is what seriously undermines its contribution to peace-building and soft security challenges. And this is where most duplication occurs, member states retaining their own hardware deployments and showing reluctance to pool efforts on such equipment. The European shortage in heavy airlift capacity is a particular constraint on deployability.

The sticking plaster approach to security

It is not merely the compromised degree of European engagement which warrants concern. The *qualitative* approach to security also appears to be drifting in the wrong direction. The guiding, progressive idea is that soft security issues can

---

5   Daniel Keohane and Claire Blommestijn, 'Strength in numbers? Comparing EU military capability in 2009 with 1999', ISS Policy Brief, European Union Institute for Security Studies, Paris, December 2009.

metastasise into hard security problems. This is the maxim that the best means to safeguard economic prosperity, social inclusion and democracy is to help universalise such goods. But in truth, the distribution of European diplomatic effort and resources tells us that the EU is back to thinking in terms of threats emanating more from strong than from weak states. A retraction in Europe's core security philosophy is under way.

EU security strategies are suffering from a worsening bout of 'liddism'. Contrary to its claim to target long-term solutions, in practice the EU is driven increasingly by the imperative of 'keeping a lid' on a whole series of pressing security preoccupations. One member state diplomat warns: 'in dealing with realist powers we have to start thinking in their terms'. In the name of such pragmatism, the EU's strategic tent can sometimes look a little too capacious, welcoming the most insalubrious of 'partners'. A whistlestop spin through some of the main strategic preoccupations of the moment shows how prevalent this trend is – and how the sticking plaster approach is increasingly the common element linking the EU's myriad security policies:

Military versus soft security cooperation
Defence deals and cooperation with security forces outstrip investment in underlying social and political problems. This is most spectacularly the case in the Middle East. Several member states have undertaken new, large-scale joint military exercises with the Egyptian armed forces. European governments have signed a plethora of new defence deals with Gulf states. We have come a long way from when the

UK directly provided security for the Trucial States of what is now the United Arab Emirates and when other sheikhdoms had the status of 'protected states'. Nevertheless, such is the extent of British defence cooperation in the Gulf today that it is the Ministry of Defence which runs the whole relationship with this region rather than the Foreign Office. The mammoth UK–Saudi Yamamah defence agreement and its current follow-on were significant for being government-to-government deals, with defence firms then subcontracted and payments made directly in oil supplies.[6] A UK Serious Fraud Office inquiry into this and a similar deal with Qatar were interrupted by the British government for fear of intelligence cooperation drying up. Liam Fox's first big speech as UK defence minister in July 2010 was all about deterrence and containment, and promised even more generous help for arms exporters to and defence ties with 'friendly' regimes (apparently cutting across the bringing together of defence, diplomacy and development in a new UK national security council, designed ostensibly to prevent these three strands undermining each other).[7]

These new security cooperation initiatives dwarf the attention paid to so-called soft security problems. Efforts to bolster fragile states remain insufficient. The EU claims that development aid is integral to security. But 2010 saw a 13 billion euro shortfall in the overall European Union

---

6 Rosemary Hollis, 'Britain and the Middle East in the 9/11 era', *Chatham House Papers*, Royal Institute of International Affairs, London, 2010, pp.160–68.

7 Chatham House, UK and the World Conference Transcript, 13 July 2010.

target to raise aid to 0.56 per cent of GDP. German, Italian, Spanish, Dutch and Irish aid fell in 2009/10, and the EU as a whole drifted further from its 0.56 commitment. Moreover, European donors still decline to pool their aid effectively, as a series of in-house reports has recognised. Europeans say that 'civilian power' is their strength. But this is now defined in such a broad way – to include such a variety of initiatives and merely the most basic of commitments to cosmopolitan norms – that it has become an almost meaningless yardstick.

Within the CSDP, proposals have gained currency for much more pre-emptive action to be taken against migrants and 'boat people'.[8] The Atalanta mission – an anti-piracy operation around the Horn of Africa – has brought in its wake a spate of EU maritime initiatives. Plans are now being discussed for six member states to upgrade naval surveillance in the Mediterranean and for a similar operation in the North Sea too. All of which resembles classical containment strategy.

In 2010 NATO has moved towards defining a new Strategic Concept. Debates related to this new doctrine reveal how European governments now seek to use NATO as protection against decline on an increasingly defensive basis. Current talks over the Strategic Concept display a striking modesty of ambition compared to the existing document drawn up in 1999. Insiders say the new doctrine is likely to have a narrower focus on core defence functions.

---

8   Alyson Bailes, 'External security policies and the European model', in Loukas Tsoukalis, 'The EU in a world in transition: fit for what purpose?', Policy Network, London, 2009, p. 33.

European security architecture

Then there is the related and vexed question of a possible new security framework with Russia. In the aftermath of the Georgian war in 2008 President Medvedev proposed a new European security pact. This would be very different from the Helsinki process, in focusing on state-to-state relations, and excluding the kinds of internal factors that the EU has argued are relevant for international security – human rights abuses, poverty, inequality, personal insecurity. In essence, the Medvedev proposal puts Russian security interests on an equal status with Western states' commitments to each other under existing security alliances.

The formal responses to Medvedev's proposal have been cautious. But while the EU may insist that it does not buy into Russia's spheres-of-influence argument, the actions of several member states suggest that they do have increasing sympathy with just such thinking. Several EU member states have indulged Russia's efforts to squeeze human rights commitments out of the OSCE, in favour of the latter body assuming a more traditional vision of hard security cooperation. They have equally lobbied against any further NATO enlargement. Some European diplomats talk of the need to court Russia as a counterbalance to China. Some policymakers even talk of prising Russia away from the other BRICs (Brazil, Russia, India, China), as an ally in decline. One Russian ambassador argues that most EU member state reactions to the Medvedev proposal demonstrate a weakened EU more desirous of Russian support, and a shift in priorities from soft to hard security. German officials argue that the EU should not have suspended dialogue within the NATO–Russian Council after Moscow's invasion of Georgia. At the end of June 2010, Angela Merkel teamed up with President Medvedev to propose a new EU–Russia security council.

Fully engaging Russia in a common European security space would buttress EU influence in relation to the broader international system. To this end, recent Russian ideas and efforts contain much merit and deserve a thoughtful EU engagement. But the risk is of agreeing to such cooperation entirely on Russia's terms. The USA has ensured that the Medvedev proposals look like a non-starter; but behind the scenes most EU member states have at least encouraged moves towards the kind of hard-security-oriented framework that Moscow desires. Russia's proposals are about increasing Russian influence over NATO, not a genuinely cooperative and comprehensive security framework for the European continent. The vision, evidently shared by several EU governments, is of pan-European hard security unity vis-à-vis a non-European world order.

The EU and Russia are now exploring the possibility of undertaking joint peacekeeping missions together. Russian officials are adamant: the improvement in EU–Russia relations during 2010 has been due to a convergence around Russia's way of seeing the world. The Medvedev pact, his officials insist, is about securing 'the entire European civilisation' against other rising powers – while also being concerned to make sure that no NATO operations occur without Russia. Europeans do not want new institutions, but Baroness Ashton has gone out of her way to say that the EU will respond positively in taking on board Russia's desire to see fundamental change in security dynamics in Europe.

This impacts on neighbouring relations. In Ukraine, the EU has shifted back to 'sharing' cooperation with Russia rather than seeking to incorporate Kiev into the norms of a collective security framework. Ukraine's new government, elected in February 2010, has adopted what it calls 'non-bloc status' and come out in favour of the Medvedev proposals. Ukrainian diplomats insist that they now think less in terms of 'EU security provisions' and more in terms of 'European security' (including Russia on an equal footing).

The signing of a new disarmament treaty in March 2010 between Russia and the USA has reinforced the conviction of Germany and some other states that the EU should fundamentally redefine its security approach towards Moscow. This is a major source of tension between member states. Russia's argument is that existing institutions do not work. But they do not work because of Russia. Again, the problem here is not so much one of pacificism, as resources and diplomatic effort focusing on the symptoms rather than the causes of security concerns.

Trying to resolve conflicts
Look also at the way in which European governments search for sticking plaster solutions in different conflict situations around the world. No CSDP deployments have been carried out actually to 'make' peace in really difficult areas involving tough political balancing. The EU's problem is in fact as much about an inability to deploy civilian personnel as the well-known weaknesses on the military side. The EAS now excludes many of the diplomats previously working at the Commission on identifying long-term means of preventing

conflicts. The European Peacebuilding Liaison Office describes the traditional diplomacy-oriented and military-heavy character of the EAS as 'realism all the way'.

In Afghanistan, the European desire is quite openly to cut a deal with the Taliban. A Spanish general reports on Spain's view that the Taliban needs to be courted even where this explicitly involves backsliding on human rights.[9] One Afghan MP complains that the West is interested only in 'a peace deal not a peace process'. France and other states have held back any massive increase in European Commission development funds to Afghanistan. This despite it being regularly pointed out that significant development assistance will be needed to provide alternative livelihoods to the reliance on heroin cultivation that sustains Taliban insurgents. There is still a feeling in European ministries that failure in Afghanistan would reflect badly on the USA but not rebound seriously on the EU's strategic credibility. It is highly likely that this may prove far too sanguine a view. Failure in Afghanistan would seriously dent US faith in European states as reliable and capable allies. A second defeat for the UK – after its humiliation in southern Iraq – would be especially damaging.

In Yemen a new 20 million euro EU counterterrorism programme has been initiated as the main response to al-Qaeda's growing presence in the country and Yemeni-trained radicals planning attacks in Europe. At the same time, the EU has supported the postponement of elections in the name of helping the autocratic Saleh regime take on

9 *El País*, 17 January 2010, p. 7.

al-Qaeda – despite Yemen's violence stemming from the government's repression of southern tribes since its victory in the civil war. European governments' narrow focus on 'defeating' al-Qaeda obscures the underlying reasons for Yemen's instability.

In Sudan, the EU has paid for a large chunk of the African Union's involvement in trying to stem the horrific Darfur conflict, without winning any political traction in return. Most European Commission aid has been held back because the Sudanese government rejected basic human rights and peace-related principles in the Cotonou accord (which is the main framework agreement governing the EU's relations with sub-Saharan Africa). But member states have colluded to fill the funding gap through their own bilateral aid, circumventing those supposedly core rights-based principles at the heart of EU security policy. Such has been the overwhelming desire to retain good relations with the Khartoum government that several member states have even leant on the ruling party in southern Sudan not to push for independence at a referendum planned, under a previous peace deal, for 2011. An EU electoral mission stated the obvious – that Sudan's April 2010 elections fell way short of being free and fair, yet EU policy continued on a course of business as usual in fear of the central government pulling out of the peace agreement.

The Arab–Israeli conflict

The Palestinian question is perhaps the most striking instance of hopes that the EU could provide a leading contribution to peace being dashed. Efforts to provide incentives to Israel for more flexible positions in peace talks have failed to have any impact. EU officials in Jerusalem admit that the Israelis treat them as 'pointless'. In the aftermath of Israel's January 2009 military incursion into the Gaza strip the EU broke off talks over a new enhanced cooperation agreement with Israel. But this move has done little to influence Israel. Even as Israeli positions have hardened under the current centre-right government, many member states remain reluctant to impose any kind of sanctions. The Commission has looked at areas of trade policy that require only qualified majority voting (QMV) to invoke sanctions. But at a political level there is still reluctance to take action, with the Italian, Polish, Czech and German governments most opposed to punitive measures against Israel.

It is not certain what leverage the EU has. It has often been suggested that the deployment of an EU force might reassure both sides sufficiently to unlock political talks. But the Israelis say they would have little confidence that a CSDP mission would provide for their security. They point to the fact that the European-led UN mission in Lebanon has stood by while Hizbollah has tripled its supply of arms.

A running sore between the EU and Israel has been that the latter fails to respect even the more technical aspects of its trade and cooperation accords with the Union. This has been so in particular in relation to the export into European markets of goods produced in Israeli settlements that the EU condemns as illegal. For several years, the EU has admitted that such goods should not benefit from trade preferences granted to Israel. And yet they continue to do so. The report of a fact-finding mission that took place to look at this question in spring 2010 is now under consideration. But governments remain cautious beyond a modest tightening up of screening procedures for Israeli goods coming into the EU. Despite frequently restating the view that the settlements are illegal they have not been willing to declare goods from those settlements ineligible for entry into European markets. The EU has, moreover, not supported the Palestinian boycott of such goods.

Increasingly, behind the scenes the EU has pushed for Saudi Arabia to take the lead role in the peace process, often on conditions contradicting its own stipulations. The EU has gone out on a limb to provide aid, loans and a trade agreement to Syria, yet in return has got almost no strategic influence in terms of convincing Damascus to move against its more radical client groups in the region. An autumn 2009 EU statement was more pro-Palestinian, and sharply rebuked by Israel. But it stopped short of recognising east Jerusalem categorically as the capital of a future Palestinian state – with the states that reined back the original Swedish presidency draft on this question earning the opprobrium of the Palestinians.

The cancellation of a big Euro-Mediterranean summit in June 2010, because Arab governments refused to sit down with Israel's hardline foreign minister, once again demonstrated the limited conciliatory pull of EU initiatives. Israeli diplomats complained that the cancellation of this summit demonstrates that the EU cannot be considered any kind of serious player and that in pre-summit talks it hardly seemed bothered whether or not the meeting went ahead as its focus was on the euro crisis.

Europe is the biggest donor to the Palestinians. The Commission now gives a sizeable 500 million euros a year, with several member states also providing generous aid programmes to the Occupied Territories. But little positive political influence flows from these funds. The EU has been limited to funding a feckless Fatah elite – the very same corrupt group that has clung to power and unleashed the division within Palestinian society that has handicapped peace talks.

The EU has even backed President Abbas's repeated postponements of elections. Indeed, not only has the EU not pushed for the holding of (now significantly delayed) presidential elections, but also decided not to take a critical stance on the postponement of municipal elections in July 2010 – after Hamas had announced a boycott and campaigning was mired by familiar Fatah intimidation.

European governments have excluded themselves from having any direct sway over Hamas, which runs the Gaza Strip. The violent and racist positions of this increasingly popular organisation are rightfully of serious concern. But it is difficult to see how European governments, by refusing to deal with the democratically elected Hamas government, can foster moderation and the kind of reform necessary for long-term peace. Diplomats now say it was a mistake to have supported the elections in 2006 (which brought Hamas to power) prior to agreement on a party law that would have excluded Hamas. Officials admit that all attempts to help build proto-state institutions in Gaza have ceased. The EU has dispatched two missions to train police and monitor the border between Gaza and Egypt. But the first of these has simply empowered rampant Fatah militia and gradually relaxed its focus on the rule of law, while the second has not even been able to operate because of Israeli objections.

The Commission has relaunched some elements of its long-term institution-building programme in the West Bank, after this was largely suspended during the second intifada. The main focus, however, is still on emergency humanitarian aid, with more than half the total aid budget going to Gaza. The problem now is not just the funding of corrupt Fatah elites: the current government is a largely technocratic one that Fatah cadres are themselves uneasy with. Rather, the problem is that these technocrats are not elected and lack broader social legitimacy. But with the choice between Fatah and Hamas, officials say there is no other option but to support trusted technocrats committed to governance reforms. Moreover, diplomats insist that what really holds back institution-building is not the no-contact rule vis-à-vis Hamas (these rules do allow contact with civil servants), but the Israeli blockade of Gaza. In their recent visits, European ministers and officials have begun to exert more pressure on Israel to lift the blockade, but they still decline openly to meet Hamas representatives. Certainly, whichever way the EU turns in this conflict, its influence is blocked by intransigents on both sides.

Iran and nuclear proliferation

Nothing is pushing the EU back to traditional forms of security thinking more than the issue of nuclear proliferation, as this raises its head with a vengeance in the new world order. The EU formally has pushed harder on non-proliferation and the export of small arms, in both cases through new conditionality clauses in its agreements with other states. But the commitment to multilateralism in non-proliferation is not without its limits. Funds to the International Atomic Energy Agency have been frozen. The UK and France were the laggards in the 2010 NPT review, in resisting firm timelines for reductions in nuclear arsenals. These two nuclear powers find themselves caught in a Catch-22: they are reluctant to give up their deterrent while the world appears so hostile; but that hostility grows as long as the big powers hang on to such privileges as possessing nuclear weapons they would deny to others.

Moreover, in the case of Iran, Europe has been left floundering. The charge made against European negotiations with Iran is that they have extended good faith and patience to the point of weak inaction. The prospect that Iran might one day possess a nuclear bomb could unsettle a whole series of delicate power balances in the Middle East. The broader durability of the NPT would be thrown into question. The sheer number of centrifuges Iran has put in place is well in excess of what would be needed for a purely civilian programme. Evidence has been found of plutonium production, underground shafts have been built at nuclear installations, army involvement has increased in the programme, and designs have been uncovered for missile re-entry vehicles and new types of warheads. Iran has tested a new long-range missile. All these facts cast doubt on Iran's insistence that its nuclear programme is intended only for civilian use. Even if Iran were to stop short of actually developing nuclear weapons, merely the knowledge of its capability to do so may have uncertain effects.

For a period in the mid-2000s, this appeared to be a case of successful European influence, as Germany, France and the UK convinced the Iranian regime to suspend uranium enrichment in return for a package of new cooperation. Since Iran broke this agreement and began an enrichment programme in earnest, the EU and its member states have bent over backwards to keep open the path of positive persuasion. While the EU has imposed four rounds of sanctions on Iran, these measures have been relatively limited in their reach. European trade and investment in Iran have not been entirely hampered.

In June 2010 the EU agreed on additional sanctions that signal the prospect of more sweeping measures. Until now sanctions have been limited to entities and officials directly implicated in the nuclear programme (a recent example includes shipping companies transporting material used in the programme). Not only have European governments given no consideration to the option of complete economic sanctions, but they have refrained even from comprehensively targeting affiliates of the Revolutionary Guard that oversee large swathes of the economy and feed into state coffers. After Iran's resumption of uranium enrichment no decision was taken to act against those Iranian banks conducting many of their international transactions in euros. No attempt was made to choke off either Iran's gas sales abroad or the country's import of refined petroleum, upon which it relies heavily.

But the June 2010 package may begin to reverse some of these areas of reticence. The EU decision was agreed as a set of measures additional to the latest UN sanctions agreed a week earlier, which do not significantly extend action against Iran. During the year prior to the decision, the EU had been reluctant to contemplate its own widened sanctions outside the United Nations, as China and Russia delayed further multilateral measures against Iran. A February 2010 internal EU paper did for the first time intimate at possible measures to choke off Iran's access to currency reserves held abroad, ban export credit guarantees for sales to Iran, prohibit gas deliveries into the country, and even efforts to target the use of commercial middlemen abusing the spirit of such measures. But, at this stage, most governments, and indeed Catherine Ashton herself, insisted that they were more cautious about taking measures beyond what could be agreed at the United Nations. So the June 2010 package seems to represent a notable change of policy. The EU is now for the first time threatening to restrict investment in the oil and gas sector and companies linked to the Revolutionary Guard. It remains to be seen if these sanctions are fully implemented in the months ahead.

Emanuele Ottolenghi makes the case for extending sanctions even further, insisting that Europe has real commercial leverage that it has been unwilling to deploy because of a fixation on short-term economic interests. The EU remains by a margin Iran's main trading partner. Forty per cent of Iran's imports come from Europe; about 25 per cent of its exports go to Europe. A large number of German and Italian companies in particular are present in Iran. Iran depends on European technology for the much-needed development of its oil and gas sector, especially liquefied natural gas (LNG) infrastructure. Many European supplies and investments are, even if unwittingly, shoring up the economic interests of the Revolutionary Guard.

Several big European energy companies – Total, Eni, Repsol, Shell, OMV, EGL – have shares in various development phases of key gas fields in Iran. These phases await implementation, as many of the companies prevaricate over whether they are indeed willing to proceed. Their withdrawal would be catastrophic for Iran.[10] And yet even after the June 2010 package, European investments have not been completely cut off. In 2010 Siemens, Eni and Allianz announced they were freezing investments or some planned operations in Iran. BP, Shell and Total expressed reluctance to proceed with contracts and ceased gasoline exports to Iran. But these decisions were not a response to European governmental strictures.

The European unease – even after the June 2010 decision – over acting more punitively can be explained by a clear preference for engagement. This position is perfectly sensible. But such engagement appears to have been expertly manipulated by the Iranian regime. Indeed, the conservative clerics have used the nuclear negotiations as a means of bolstering their own position against Iran's pro-democracy opposition forces. Europe's cautious line is that the nuclear and democracy issues should be kept separate, as pressure on the regime for human rights improvements will make it feel more threatened and thus more determined to proceed with its nuclear programme.

---

10 Emanuele Ottolenghi, *Under a Mushroom Cloud: Europe, Iran and the Bomb*, Profile Books, London, 2009.

The EU–Iran human rights dialogue was effectively wound up in 2004. Since then many new incentives have been offered to Iran without any link to resumed cooperation on human rights. Nobel Prize-winning human rights activist Shirin Ebadi has been critical of European companies for shoring up the regime. German politicians and diplomats are quite adamant: we need Supreme Leader Khamenei for a nuclear deal; political change will not slow the nuclear programme; and, anyway, if we withdraw from engagement, the Chinese will simply fill the vacuum. Germany has been strongly criticised by Israel for being so soft on President Ahmadinejad, a Holocaust denier who would be locked up within Germany itself.

As protests have raged in Iran since the elections of June 2009 the EU has offered an implicit trade-off: no pressure on a reeling Iranian regime in return for the latter compromising on its nuclear programme. The EU did not even extend its list of visa bans on Iranian officials after the violence of 2009. In that year the EU also negotiated an association agreement with Syria, in the hope of Damascus acting as a bridge to Tehran – this as Syria was arresting another group of human rights activists in late 2009.

James Rubin has pointed out that during the Cold War the West negotiated with Russia on arms control while also seeking to provide support to dissidents, making it look unduly defeatist to have concluded that the same cannot be tried in Iran.[11] The longer Iran holds out against a deal the

---

11 James Rubin, 'The principle of the thing', *Newsweek*, 5 December 2009.

more many in the West will conclude that political change is a solution – rather than a danger – to a nuclear settlement. The fact that protests have spread beyond a small liberal elite makes the EU's delinking of the nuclear and human rights questions look even more short sighted. Protests have spread to the working class, but Europe remains nervous at being associated 'only' with a group of 'Western-style liberals'.

The argument is often made that democratisation would not solve the nuclear problem to the extent that opponents of the regime support Iran's right to develop a nuclear programme. This is true. But it is also the case that opposition candidate Mir Hossein Mousavi stated in the 2009 campaign that he would change Ahmadinejad's 'wild and irresponsible' foreign policy. While Western governments fear that internal instability may harden the regime's line in nuclear negotiations, the inverse dynamic is that the growing popularity of reformers is undercutting the consensus in favour of a hard line on the nuclear dossier.[12] The Iranian regime fears isolation, not slightly tightened restrictions on members of the government inner circle – yet the latter is precisely the limit of European political will.

Arguably, Europe has been too absolute on the nuclear issue, too indulgent of human rights abuses. A rebalancing is required: more flexible solutions to the nuclear impasse should be explored, while Iran's domestic political pathologies should not been seen as quite such expendable negotiating capital. This is not to advocate any kind of aggressive

---

12 Farideh Farhi, 'Ahmadinejad's nuclear folly', *Middle East Report*, 252, Autumn 2009, pp. 2–5.

support for 'regime change', but a more holistic way of understanding the security challenges that Iran presents. The EU should not sacrifice courageous Iranian democrats on the altar of its own immediate security aims.

Conclusion

This chapter has run through some of the main security issues confronting Europe. Without going into exhaustive detail on any single issue, it has sought to extract the common trend that can be witnessed in European policies – in terms of the EU's general level of commitment to international security, its approach to the shape of new security treaties, its conflict resolution policies and the specific example of dealing with Iran's nuclear programme. This common trend is that of EU security policy being an uneasy amalgam of power-balancing, bandwagoning alliances and free-riding.

Many commentators insist that the UK and France, in particular, still need to draw back in their international security reach.[13] Much hubris does indeed require deflating. But significant retraction is not the way forward. Europe is right to have a measured and modest idea of what it can achieve. But peace and security cannot be defined as isolation. As Churchill often warned: fail to confront uncomfortable truths in the name of short-term ease and you will reap the very conflict you set out to avoid. Or, in Byron's metaphor, 'today's smiles form the channels of a future tear'. The EU is increasingly a security free-rider. It should at least

---

13 Simon Jenkins, 'Naval nostalgia and edgy kit is no basis for a sane defence', *Guardian*, 8 April 2010.

pull its weight as a navigating co-pilot. Epicurean detachment is not the way to confront decline.

The current drift in policy is unlikely to provide for security on a sustainable basis. A high-profile and innovative 'security jam' consultation between diplomats, military officers and experts produced a sobering conclusion in mid-2010: instead of liberal security norms being spread from the West to the rest of world, today there is more 'reverse socialisation' of strategic realism from rising powers into Europe and North America.[14] Instability can be outwardly contained, but without heading off the prospect of greater risk in the longer term: a copper wire appears an effortless conductor – until it overloads and snaps. Moreover, the EU offers an overly sanitised view that insecurity is 'out there', while security depends on what 'we' do to 'them', at a government-to-government level. In fact it depends on the nature of two-way social and economic interactions, the strategic impact of which the EU increasingly neglects.

The security challenge is not that of defending against rising powers, but enticing the latter into cooperative security frameworks. The EU must think more geostrategically about its international partnerships. But strategic vision is not synonymous with classical security realpolitik. Did not balance-of-power thinking – such as is now returning – end up in the carnage of the early twentieth century? Europeans might seriously ponder on the danger of forgetting history's lessons.

14 Jonathan Holslag and David Henry Doyle, 'The new global security landscape: 10 recommendations from the 2010 Security Jam', a Security and Defence Agenda Report, 2010, p. 45.

4
European identity and global decline

The challenges facing Europe extend beyond traditional state-to-state security issues. A key set of questions relates to how the perceived infection of instability from outside in the form of migration and radicalism increasingly impinges upon internal security. Many increasingly see Europe's internal problems and uneasy ethnic mix as sapping its power in the world. It is not only in the classic security sense but also on a social plane that Europe appears to be on the back foot. Unfavourable demographics, migration, Muslim radicalism and uncertainties over Europe's cultural identity can all seem to fuse into the same picture of decline.

The tight interconnection of all these issues lends particular gravity to Europe's plight. Indeed, these different concerns are now invariably conflated in the European psyche into a single cluster of doom. The prominence of this nexus between Islamic radicalism, migration and the flailing 'European identity' has probably done more than anything else to ensure that fear is the dominant emotion when Europe looks out on to the emerging world order. It is this nexus which has engendered the most hyperbolic talk of 'the end of Europe' and the continent's 'cultural death'.

And in response a siege mentality has taken hold against the variation in values and conflictive identities pressing in from beyond the gates of the European citadel. Rather than seeking to refashion an identity that holds universal appeal, which adapts to change within Europe while also providing a platform for external credibility, the EU seeks to freeze-frame an idealised identity. This is not a feasible strategy for managing decline. The EU is tilting too far towards seeing diversity as a problem rather than an asset in the post-Western world.

Identity wars

An increasingly prevalent view is that Europe's lack of firm belief in its own values is leading to over-tolerance of non-European, and especially Islamic, customs, and that this hastens European decline. A spate of books and essays now posits this same essential thesis. They contend that Europe is weakened by the sheer volume of Muslim immigration. The number of Muslim arrivals is now seen to be so large – in most member states foreign-born populations will rise to around 30 per cent by 2050 – that a qualitative shift has occurred compared to previous immigration. It is widely asserted that European Islam is a forceful and self-confident religion that thrives on the self-loathing secularism of Europe's 'native' population. Family reunification policies and higher Muslim birth rates are now the two main factors pushing up the proportion of the immigrant population.

Muslim populations are said to be moving farther away from core European values rather than gradually assimilating. Even those sought out as the charismatic voices of a European Islam – such as Tariq Ramadan – are unapologetic in their assertion that Islamic values are and must be ascendant against a decadent and failing set of Western values. Their Islam may be 'moderate', but it is unashamedly fashioned as a means of resisting and supplanting prevalent 'European values'. The widespread charge is that European governments have been too accepting of this. Christopher Caldwell aims his fire at a string of European laws that attempt to offer protection against 'incitement to religious hatred' – laws that rub up awkwardly against liberal freedoms. These laws protect Islam even against the kind of satire and humour that European liberals themselves used to rein in the power of the Christian Church.[1]

Christopher Hitchens insists that the indulgence of religious rights is Europe's 'cultural suicide', as religion unavoidably menaces the live-and-let-live liberalism on which European values are supposedly predicated.[2] Bernard-Henri Lévy makes a similar case that today's Left has become too tolerant of Muslim rights in a way that threatens the secular polity's notion of liberal freedoms.[3] Walter Laqueur's widely read thesis that we are witnessing 'the last days of Europe' argues that European governments have been too generous in offering positive discrimination in housing, education and employment, and have been overly permissive of

1   Christopher Caldwell, *Reflections on the Revolution in Europe: Immigration, Islam and the West*, Random House, New York, 2009.
2   Christopher Hitchens, *God Is Not Great: How Religion Poisons Everything*, Twelve Books, New York, 2007, p. 33.
3   Bernard-Henri Lévy, *Left in Dark Times: A Stand Against the New Barbarism*, Random House, New York, 2009, chapter 6.

'exceptionalism' in respect for migrants' cultural sensitivities. This applies, he contends, even to those like Nicolas Sarkozy seen as 'tough' on migrants.[4]

Such sceptics insist that Islam is not a mere epiphenomenon that flows from social or economic grievances; and yet European politicians go to extraordinary lengths to avoid attaching any blame at all to what they rather confidently identify as 'the real Islam'. Critics say that the creation of official state Muslim bodies in European countries is desperate futility.

Academics have charted the shift from an 'outward-looking and cosmopolitan European identity' towards an 'inward-looking, national-populist European identity project', with 'traditional chauvinistic nationalism ... now donning a European mantle'.[5] The general assumption is that the UK model of multiculturalism has failed most spectacularly, as member states shift more towards the French concept of fostering and demanding a single cultural template.

The opposing, and more convincing, view to that of the sceptics is that Europe has stuck too inflexibly to an unchanging and fiercely secular identity. Perhaps, mulls Timothy Garton Ash, 'the offensive secularism of European society is not an asset but rather a liability for Europe's soft power'. Policy based on defining Europe in adversarial

4   Walter Laqueur, *The Last Days of Europe: Epitaph for an Old Continent*, St Martin's Press, New York, 2007.

5   Jeffrey Checkel and Peter Katzenstein, 'The politicization of European identities', in Jeffrey Checkel and Peter Katzenstein (eds), *European Identity*, Cambridge University Press, Cambridge, 2009, pp. 11 and 13.

fashion against a religiously fired 'other' equates to a Euronationalism that, he fears, is doomed to failure.[6] In his moving journey through Europe's twentieth-century history, Geert Mak reaches the conclusion that 'One can wonder whether there is any sense at all to the discussion concerning "European identity", whether it is not in fact diametrically opposed to the entire history of the "European concept".[7]

In similar vein, Dario Castiglione perceptively notes that there is simply too much variety within Europe to be shoehorned into a single European identity, as German philosopher Jürgen Habermas and others have sought to do. Habermas sees a universalist identity moving away from national interests to citizens' belief in European constitutional values. But the identity he posits – based around a common secularism – can only be his own particularist set of preferences, not shared by many across Europe. Castiglione suggests that what *can* convincingly be said to be central to European identity is the role of open politics in allowing the expression of such variety. Vibrant democratic process is what should bind, not particular prescriptions for a manufactured European identity.[8]

The foremost expert on political Islam, Olivier Roy, made the celebrated suggestion that Muslim grievances can be

---

6 Timothy Garton Ash, *Facts Are Subversive: Political Writing from a Decade without a Name*, Atlantic Books, London, 2009, pp. 77 and 126.

7 Geert Mak, *In Europe: Travels through the Twentieth Century*, Vintage Books, London, 2007, p. 486.

8 Dario Castiglione, 'Political identity in a community of strangers', in Checkel and Katzenstein, op. cit.

explained by Marx, not Muhammad. Even if he may have gone a little too far in this assertion, he did capture the sense that Muslims are not driven by qualitatively different forces. Many polls report that Muslim minorities already define themselves as European and support the same secular principles of state–religion separation as other groups.[9]

The question of tolerating intolerance is one of the most vexed facing Europe today as it struggles to fashion a modern identity. There is a clear need to avoid *both* militant extremes. On the one hand, that of militant secularism and assimilation programmes aimed at squashing religion out of the system. Freedom of speech must not be compromised but subtle and respectful ways must be found of bringing Muslims into the mainstream. On the other hand, public policy must not cede priority to group rights, as has happened often merely in the name of political correctness. It is not only the majority which must adapt to respect the minority. Philosopher John Rawls made the seminal argument that individual rights lie at the heart of a core concept of liberal values that is undiscriminating to group identities.

It may be that the UK and some other member states had moved too far in the latter direction of differentiated cultural rights. The UK and others have widened blasphemy laws too far. Europe must be self-critical, not self-loathing in

---

9 Gallup World Poll: Special Report: Muslims in Europe, 2007, www.gallup.com/…/WPSRMuslimsinEurope2050707 ReligiousandNationalIdentities.pdf; Pew Global Survey report, 6 July 2006, http://pewglobal.org/2006/07/06/muslims-in-europe-economic-worries-top-concerns-about-religious-and-cultural-identity/.

its cultural identity. But the main problem lies in the other direction. France and most continental member states have gone too far in the direction of secular assimilation. Belgium has become the first European state to ban the burqah. A similar parliamentary proposal in France is before the constitutional court. Academics who have been through the fine detail of the scores of new integration programmes find that their common thread is how prohibitive they aim to be of minorities' current cultural preferences.[10]

In the Netherlands the mood is especially defensive. In 2004, the then prime minister Jan Peter Balkenende feared an overly tolerant Europe becoming a 'spiritless machine, grinding to a halt'.[11] The Dutch government is imposing language obligations on immigrants, but not those from EU states or those in the country for high-tech contracts. Southern EU states still accord religious rights around the hegemony of the Catholic Church, even as they fret about the political reach of Islam – apparently unaware of the irony. Europe struggles to maintain the distinctiveness of its social model while allowing in a large number of immigrants – for most, defending the former seems to outweigh the economic need for the latter.

The challenges of decline, identity and counterterrorism sometimes appear to have merged. To approach counterterrorism as a matter of deeper assimilation of minorities in

---

10 Sergio Carrera, 'Integration of immigrants versus social inclusion: a typology of integration programmes in the EU', in Thierry Balzacq and Sergio Carrera (eds), *Security versus Freedom? A Challenge for Europe's Future*, Ashgate, Aldershot, 2006, pp. 88 and 91.

11 Jan Peter Balkenende, speech at 'The politics of European values' conference, The Hague, 7 September 2004.

general clearly risks stoking further resentment. A natural and positive sense of national, or even European, sense of belonging is to be much desired. But not when it is artificially engineered specifically as a means, quite tendentiously, of targeting the minority community as 'the problem' for counterterrorism and in need of ideational reprimand. Many studies have shown that there is little correlation between an individual's degree of 'assimilation' and their resistance to being radicalised.

There is a thin line between rooting out potentially violent beliefs and seeking to influence values that simply sit uneasily with majority norms. Many current integration and national identity programmes unduly blur this line. The French government has pushed the most expansive concept of such identity programmes, including at the European level during its 2008 EU presidency. While it has to some extent been reined back by other member states, the trend is still in its preferred direction.

Muslims protesting in London at the cartoon images of the Prophet published in the Danish press carried placards proclaiming 'Freedom go to hell!' Unfortunately, many European governments seemed to side with these hotheads and follow exactly this advice. Even if Muslim communities were today more anti-Western than native populations are Islamophobic, tackling fire with fire cannot be a fruitful way to proceed. Security in an uncertain and fast-changing world is best obtained by more not less space for personal autonomy: it is this which eases tensions.

Tolerance and international standing

Much of what is written by the anti-multiculturalists is undoubtedly inflammatory and distasteful. The purpose of this book is not to delve into such trends and tensions within Europe itself. Rather, it is concerned with Europe's *international* standing and influence, rather than with the level of immigration into Europe per se or debates over the integration of minority communities within each European state. It is on the internal–external link that much less has been said, and in relation to which much of what is proffered is often reflexive and lazy.

The crucial link in terms of European *foreign* policy is that growing multiculturalism is seen by many to weaken Europe not only internally but beyond its borders too. Luminaries such as Bernard Lewis have suggested that the expansion of Muslim minorities means that the Middle East and Muslim Asia will soon be dictating terms to Europe on key international and strategic questions. Many commentators see Islam as inherently threatening to European international power.

Muslim communities are often said to have a fundamentally different view of the world to the native population, and one that is pernicious to traditional 'European values'. Christopher Caldwell argues that the new fashion of using Europe's multiculturalism as a basis for inter-religious dialogue with Muslim countries only benefits the religious in a continent whose values are now fundamentally at odds with religion. In similar vein, Bruce Thornton sees Europe's pursuit of such forms of dialogue with the Middle East and the broader Muslim world as an 'appeasement' festering at the root of the continent's 'slow-motion suicide'.[12]

European Islam, some insist, has not been strongly supportive of the more liberal and reformist strands of political Islam in the Middle East and North Africa. The sceptics' charge is that Muslim populations in Europe do not help promote a foreign policy of universalism and cultural understanding; they simply force Europe to adopt pro-Arab causes and bend to the will of Middle Eastern dictatorships.[13] Politicians from many Muslim-dominated constituencies now have to adopt 'Arab nationalist' causes to placate their voters, in a way that cannot further Europe's longer-term interest in a balanced sense. In the Danish cartoon imbroglio, Europe's Muslims clearly sided with the angry protesters in Karachi and Cairo more than with their fellow Europeans' defence of the freedom of speech.

The fact that Europe has let in so many Muslims is, critics argue, interpreted in the rest of the world as weakness not strength – a reflection of European guilt for previous misdemeanours, from a society in terminal decline. Caldwell, again, points to what he sees as the defeatism evident in the decision to excise from the EU's new constitutional treaty all mention of Christianity in deference to the feelings of the Arab world.[14] Europe preaches tolerance and multiculturalism; in response Arab regimes deliver a humiliating slap in the face by restricting Christian minority rights. When European governments refer to the need to address the 'root

---

12 Bruce Thornton, *Decline and Fall: Europe's Slow-motion Suicide*, Encounter Books, New York, 2007, pp. 89 and 91.

13 Caldwell, op. cit., pp. 144–6.

14 Ibid., p. 161.

causes of terrorism' and understand the grievances that drive it, this is interpreted in the Arab world as Europe holding up its hands and saying 'we were wrong; we are to blame; we must change more than you'.

The truculent critics who make this case undoubtedly raise some highly valid points that are uncomfortable to those espousing liberal ideals. They provide an invaluable service in rooting out some of the mush of political correctness. Yet it cannot be convincing to argue that, at root, Europe's tolerance internally is a source of impotence externally. Showing less tolerance to minorities within Europe cannot be a sensible way of managing relative decline. Indeed, quite the opposite response is required. There are a number of reasons why this is so.

First, a key source of European influence, the aspirational appeal of its basic values, is compromised when these values fail – not when they are deepened. In interviews with Islamist representatives in the Arab world a constantly raised point is that hostility to Europe in the Middle East is nourished by the lack of full integration of Muslim communities within European states.[15] Europeans might feel such arguments are exaggerated and self-serving. But the extent to which European governments seem intent on ignoring such perceptions is increasingly disquieting.

Asked about Europe's foreign policy influence, one high-ranking Indonesian diplomat, involved in many of the

---

15 Michael Emerson and Richard Youngs (eds), *Political Islam and European Foreign Policy*, Centre for European Policy Studies and Fundación para las Relaciones Internacionales y el Diálogo Exterior, Brussels and Madrid, 2007.

counterterrorism programmes offered by European governments, makes this connection immediately: the EU is losing
its previous advantage over the USA in terms of perceived
tolerance levels towards Islam. That the desperate raft-borne
arrivals on European soil are often allowed to stay in contravention of formal immigration rules is surely something to
welcome, not bemoan, as so much commentary now does
– a gesture of necessary humanity underpinning Europe's
international image.

Second, Muslim minorities have in some cases become
firm advocates of liberal values being given a stronger – not
weaker – place within EU foreign policy. One should not be
naive: to argue, with those at the other end of the spectrum,
that Islam automatically offers a means of reviving moral
values that have been sullied and abandoned in the West
is equally simplistic. In general, European Muslim groups
have not been that active in engaging on EU foreign policy.
But positive potential clearly exists. The EU institutions
and member-state governments have in fact used European
Muslim groups in an increasingly systematic way to facilitate and catalyse their myriad cultural dialogues across
the Arab world. Take a look at the positions adopted and
advocacy undertaken by a group like the Federation of
Islamic Organisations in Europe and the human rights
dimension is striking. It is Europe's most right-wing anti-
immigrant parties which are often warmest towards Middle
Eastern dictatorships and their efforts to suppress Islam.
Interestingly, in 2010 the Commission and European Parliament have initiated a project with Muslim leaders on how
Europe should respond to the economic crisis in a way that

safeguards social solidarity and international legitimacy.[16] Such initiatives, however, are still few in number, the exception rather than the rule.

Third, minority communities can help strengthen economic ties with their respective home states. This has been a great source of strength for the USA. Remittances from migrant workers in Europe are also several times larger than official European aid flows. This is a form of boosting development efforts that the EU ritually insists are key to attenuating security threats and instability. These remittances in turn facilitate trade and investment between Europe and developing markets.

A balance must clearly be found. But policy tips increasingly too far towards the exclusionary. Assimilation programmes are asking migrants to imbibe an imaginary set of nationalist ideals far more than they promote the kind of post-national cosmopolitanism that European sees itself as standing for in world affairs. As more restrictions are being placed on the veil, research shows that such moves have done more than anything else to lower the esteem in which 'European values' are held by citizens in North Africa and the Middle East. The now notorious French law requiring education to extol the positive virtues of France's colonial record in North Africa is exactly the wrong way to create the basis of goodwill requisite to achieve foreign policy goals.

Efforts to perpetuate the influence of European culture look increasingly ridiculous. Spain's Iberoamerican

16 See the website of the Federation of the Islamic Organisations in Europe, available at http://www.euro-muslim.com/En_default.aspx.

community, the UK's continuing investment in the Commonwealth, Paris's emphasis on *Francophonie* all fail to resonate with their target populations – indeed, the latter see such initiatives as arrogant relics of the colonial period and evidence of Europe's failure to think anew about the future. In sum, as diversity increases Europe needs to rethink its own model and recognise that no longer does the same fixed 'boundary' fall between Europe and the outside world.

Radicalism: what message to the rest of the world?

The crucial link to the subject matter of this book is that the confusion over identity questions infects European foreign policy with discriminatory defensiveness. This is seen clearly in EU attempts to deal with international terrorism and 'global jihad'. For several years EU member states have discussed the threat of Islamist radicalisation. They have waxed lyrical on the need to appreciate the international injustices that drive acts of violence and terrorism. But little concrete action has followed. Increasingly the feeling is that a Europe chastened by the unpredictability of the Muslim world can best 'leave alone'.

The focus in EU policies is now overwhelmingly on choking off radicalisation within Europe itself. Diplomats reveal that policy debates are now directed almost exclusively at internal integration programmes. This has led to confusion in respect of the internal–external dichotomy. No common European voice has been heard on the thorny question of defamation in the Muslim world, for instance. Hundreds of new positive discrimination initiatives within Europe have no counterpart within the EU's external relations. Attempts to assist social modernisation in North Africa, the Middle East and South-East Asia as part of the counterterrorism agenda have atrophied – where they have not been aborted altogether. The EU's search for this kind of strategic carapace can only be illusory.

EU governments have to date agreed three major packages of counterterrorist measures which all focus primarily on strengthening law enforcement and monitoring measures. Although European governments rejected President Bush's 'war on terror' and differences have recently deepened over data sharing, behind the scenes their security agencies have worked with the USA to render more robust the defence against terrorism. Europol has been handed new powers. Many more suspects have been detained in the European Union than in the USA. Both the UK and France have empowered national intelligence councils.

Such measures have, of course, engendered understandably concerned comment on 'the loss of civil liberties'. Although the concerns are legitimate, some tend towards exaggerated sensationalism. In many EU member states court rulings have begun to roll back some of the worst excesses of the control orders, stop-and-search provisions and financial asset freezes introduced in the panicky aftermath of the 9/11, Madrid and London attacks. The European Court of Justice has reined governments back in their extension of terrorist watch lists. The new Conservative–Liberal Democrat government in the UK has committed itself to reversing post-9/11 civil rights restrictions. The attention has turned more towards programmes of pre-emptive engagement and education as a means of preventing radicalisation in some of

Europe's increasingly tense large cities. Debates rumble on over whether such initiatives are in fact tackling the complex causes of radicalisation in the right way, but the approach has certainly become more multifaceted and sensitive.

Even if to a modest degree a better balance is being found in the EU's internal security policy, however, this does not lessen the real danger that has arisen in Europe looking inwards in its 'deradicalisation' strategies. The 'homeland security' orientation certainly makes bad politics in terms of popularising European integration: such measures are now used remorselessly by anti-EU campaign groups, as in Open Europe's attacks on the 'EU surveillance state'.

Insiders in Brussels admit that the foreign policy machinery has struggled to get a grip on the counterterrorism dossier. Led by interior ministry officials, the counterterrorism agenda has turned inwards. In mid-2010 a new EU committee was created comprising member-state representatives working specifically on internal security. Only a few dedicated individuals in Brussels and national capitals are left making the case that effective counterterrorism is a matter of investing significantly in improving the economic, political and human rights situations, and the social structures, of countries *beyond* Europe's borders. European Union counterterrorism coordinator Gilles de Kerchove and his excellent team have valiantly made this case, but have been left high and dry, with few resources or political support.

Budgets for beefing up 'homeland' defences vastly exceed those projecting European reform and counter-radicalisation efforts outwards. Look at Contest 2, the UK's counterterrorism strategy introduced in March 2009; only a tiny share of this initiative's £1 billion budget is allocated for counter-radicalisation activities outside Europe.[17] The budget of UK intelligence services runs at over £2 billion a year, while those of externally oriented reform projects amount to no more than a few million pounds. Some good initiatives have undoubtedly been carried out within the Middle East. The UK has funded local human rights organisations to monitor security services' treatment of suspects in places like Jordan and a raft of rule-of-law programmes in the tribally administered areas of Pakistan. But these are relatively few in number. In 2010, the EU has spent more on cleaning and maintenance for the European Parliament (41 million euros) than even the larger member states spend on reform-oriented deradicalisation in the Middle East.

In general, the message sent to the rest of the world is that Europe meets terrorist violence through cultural containment rather than through promoting progressive politics. The narrowing of some civil liberties within Europe has gone hand in hand with efforts to keep radicalism outside Europe at bay through very traditional security measures.

Interestingly, many European diplomats insist that it is preferable for the EU to focus on internal law enforcement issues in order to distance it from the US belief that counter-terrorism is first and foremost a foreign policy issue. While the USA might indeed tend towards excess in this conviction, the EU is as guilty of adhering just as unhelpfully to the opposite extreme. The EU's latest package of counterterrorist

---

17 Her Majesty's Government, 'Pursue, prevent, protect, prepare. Containing the terrorist threat: the UK Government's strategy', HMG, London, 2009, p. 4.

measures agreed at the end of 2009 (the so-called Stockholm programme) refers again to the importance of addressing the 'external dimension' to the internal struggle against radicalism and organised crime. But one searches this lengthy new work plan in vain for anything that would give greater concrete operational meaning to this link.

Meetings in Brussels on the external dimensions of counterterrorism began only in 2008. To date they have not advanced beyond basic information-sharing. In April 2010, the Dutch intelligence service launched a new initiative to focus on external policy, recognising that all its focus had hitherto been on internal radicalism[18] – a correct observation of policy imbalance, but a mistaken prescription for thinking that the solution is primarily through security-services-led foreign policy.

In their dealings with governments around the world, European states virtually never make a serious issue out of the extremely repressive treatment meted out to terrorist suspects. Indeed, massive amounts of weaponry are now channelled from Europe to the security forces of these countries in the name of cooperation on counterterrorism. And advice and assistance are now even taken from Middle Eastern regimes to monitor their respective citizens within Europe. One Muslim democracy activist complains angrily that European support for so-called security-sector reforms is being remilitarised: 'you are paying regimes to kill people not prevent radicalism'.

Indeed, the EU now most commonly works with the likes

---

18 *Financial Times*, 21 April 2010, p. 6.

of Pakistan, Algeria, Egypt and others to see how its own recent experience in tightening border controls and surveillance measures can be extended to these sites of radicalism. Partner countries are even threatened with having the offer of new cooperation agreements with the EU withdrawn should they reject such cooperation. It would seem rather unnecessary to make such a threat to the kind of governments that are hardly likely to reject offers of outside help to clamp down even further against their internal opponents ... a bit like bullying an alcoholic to drink up more quickly. Indeed, the whole notion of Europe helping to beef up the internal security capacities of states like Egypt or Saudi Arabia might be likened to plying the drunk with even more spirits.

The British Parliament's Human Rights Committee caused a furore by suggesting that UK security cooperation, in particular with Pakistani and Saudi Arabian security services, has left the government conniving in torture.[19] The European Parliament frequently returns to its increasing concern that development aid is being used for building up security forces. Arab regimes' promises not to torture suspects returned to their shores from Europe have turned out to be worth nothing – as European governments presumably knew would be the case.

And neither have European governments fulfilled their repeated promises to engage with Islamist opposition forces across the Muslim world. Our research in FRIDE found that

---

19 House of Commons Foreign Affairs Committee, 'Human Rights Report 2008', 7th Report of Session 2008–09, House of Commons, London, July 2009.

such parties and movements have had little contact with European diplomats. They are still excluded from European support programmes. They rarely count on European backing when their members are periodically rounded up by security forces. They complain that when they are included in discussions these tend to be vacuous talking-shops that 'talk down' to Islamists. They rail that Europe is targeting them with public diplomacy to improve its own image, but then fails to do anything to defend their political rights.[20]

Europe's idea of helping is to send 'moderate' imams trained in Europe, while supporting the repression that accords the radical imams their popularity in the first place. A number of governments, including the current incumbents in Italy and some central European states, can still be shockingly categorical that Islam must be kept at bay in the broader Middle East, even if it takes some embarrassingly thuggish regimes to do so. All these are long-standing imbalances within European polices. But the promise was that all this would change after 9/11 and the London and Madrid bombings. It hasn't.

This does not mean that counter-radicalisation efforts are absent from EU foreign policy. But it does ensure that their scope has been too narrow to be effective. Reflecting this, a central feature of European thinking is the argument that foreign policy and security aims can be enhanced over the long term through dialogue on religious understanding. Hundreds of initiatives are now supported to foster exchanges between Christian and Muslim religious

---

20 Emerson and Youngs, op. cit.

figures. Intercultural dialogue has even become something of a central 'narrative' in EU attempts to recover lost ground in international affairs and doubts over the rationale of the integration project itself.[21] These initiatives are welcome and positive. Forums such as the Alliance of Civilisations fund many useful projects on education reform and youth exchanges.

But such efforts are misconceived as part of overarching identity-cum-strategic policy. They tend to crystallise conservative power structures, militating against the kind of modernising change that might reduce tensions in many societies. The Alliance of Civilisations has, in the words of one leading diplomat, been 'reduced to religion'. And in 2010 a lead role in coordination was handed to Egypt, allowing the latter to promote Arab human rights declarations against the universal declaration. Such initiatives tend to subordinate universal human rights claims to imagined cultural differences, in more than a small nod towards cultural relativism.

Security cannot be advanced through mushy cultural pow-wows, while political conditions continue to deteriorate across much of the Muslim world. Culturally based dialogue goes too far in assuming that spiritual identity is the motor that drives international tensions. Politics cannot be avoided in the way that such initiatives claim: many, if not most, terrorists have their provenance in strong autocratic, not failed, states. One example here is the way in which Arab regimes have intervened in and frustrated the

---

21 Sara Silvestri, 'Islam and religion in the EU political system', *West European Politics*, 32(6): 1212–39.

'cultural cooperation' work of the much-lauded Anna Lindh Foundation, the flagship cultural initiative of Europe's Mediterranean policy. This demonstrates that culture and politics cannot be separated.

In private, European diplomats despair that, with Arab regimes clamping down against their opponents, the EU has missed what was a brief post-9/11 window of opportunity to empower democratic Islamists. The Alliance of Civilisations and many other such projects see a religious cleavage between East and West, where Europe would gain influence in working more concretely to advance standard social and economic opportunity across the Muslim world. This recalls the dictum that politicians often seek plaudits by building bridges over easy terrain where no rivers rage.

The need for more political approaches is suggested by the fact that the soft power of European education has spectacularly failed on many occasions: there have been several cases of non-European nationals receiving higher education in Europe before going on to join radical groups and plot attacks against European targets. Former British foreign secretary David Miliband often acknowledged that the sharp dichotomy often drawn between moderates and radicals is overly simplistic. Yet most European foreign policy initiatives still aim rather artificially at engineering a 'moderate Islam' across the world, rather than aiming at the underlying political conditions driving radicalisation.

German Chancellor Angela Merkel has used Christianity as grounds for arguing that Turkey should be excluded from the European Union. In seeking to protect an illusory European identity, this kind of position helps create in

Turkish Muslims a reinvigorated image of the 'other'. Merkel's much-cited suggestion that Turkey's role is as a bridge, belonging neither to one side nor the other, seems entirely disingenuous in this sense. The metaphor is inappropriate anyway: how can Turkey be a bridge from Europe if it is not inside Europe? Some analysts say Turkish citizens are turning away from Europe and drifting outside its orbit of cultural influence. Turkey's impressively intellectually rooted foreign minister, Ahmet Davotoglu, warns: 'if the EU cannot get beyond uni-culturalism as its only vision for the new world order, Turkey will look for more promising avenues of safeguarding its rising power'. He talks of Turkey shifting from seeing itself as the eastern fringe of Europe to the core motor of western Asia – this reflecting the 'normalisation of history ... [beyond] ... the Eurocentric cultural era'.

Migration and existential security

The issue of immigration is one that combines all these issues of identity and security, and encapsulates the bunkering attitude that prevails in Europe's reaction to decline. Trying to capture today's combination of global markets with more restrictive border controls, academics talk of 'gated globalism'. If one accepts the term, then Europe is contributing more to building the gates than to the globalism.

Europe's relative decline and demographic imbalances breed a fear of being overwhelmed by outsiders. During the next twenty years, the population around the southern shores of the Mediterranean will increase by 100 million. Of course, a standard refrain is that, whatever cultural challenges migration may present, it is necessary to Europe's future economic prosperity. The critics of multiculturalism, however, even doubt the economic value of immigration. They insist that immigrant economic activity is largely of value to the migrant community itself. They point out that immigration can hardly be a solution to Europe's problem of an ageing society, as migrants themselves inevitably age and come to draw more on state resources.

Immigration controls are becoming more restrictive across Europe. Overall immigration into the EU increased between 2000 and 2006, before beginning to decline steadily year on year. The number of asylum seekers accepted annually into the EU has halved in the last decade.[22] In 2009, asylum rejections were two and half times the number of positive decisions.

The EU's Return Directive agreed in 2008 has caused consternation across the world and besmirched Europe's reputation and soft power. Bolivian president Evo Morales labelled it 'the directive of shame'. Even the UN has weighed in to criticise new EU readmission agreements as violating migrants' basic rights. Spain repatriated 90,000 migrant workers in 2009. It opened embassies in West Africa with the express purpose of controlling migration – Spain's aid resources going here instead of as part of a global vision for dealing with the new world order.

The EU's new Pact of Immigration and Asylum is critical of any regularisation of irregular workers. It commits to removing illegal migrants immediately, and to do this through cooperation between member states on carrying

---

22 Eurostat, *Data in Focus – 18/2010*, p. A13.

out expulsions and border patrols. The EU's new Migration Management Support Fund orientates its funds overwhelming towards the security aspects of migration rather than dealing with its developmental and human rights root causes. The EU has actually worked with and paid the Moroccan government to set up a unit for border surveillance. It is difficult to imagine an example of more direct exclusionary control.

Entry and exit controls at EU borders have been strengthened. New Rapid Border Interventions Teams have been set up. The EU's borders agency, Frontex, has been vastly empowered. Its budget increased from 5 million euros in 2005 to 70 million in 2008. In May 2010, Frontex congratulated itself on having used naval patrols and its now nearly half a million border guards to ensure a significant year-on-year reduction in attempted illegal crossings into Europe.[23]

Revealingly, around 60 per cent of the EU's overall budget for 'Freedom, Security and Justice' is now spent on controlling migrations.[24] Frontex has itself negotiated new agreements on the return of migrants, notably with North African states, Afghanistan and Iraq. In the Mediterranean the EU has allocated 1.82 billion euros for border control for 2007–13, several times in excess of funding for tackling the developmental drivers of migration. The development aid budgets of most member states now fund programmes quite instrumentally aimed at choking off migration more than at genuinely promoting poverty reduction.

---

23 *Guardian*, 25 May 2010.
24 For figures, see Commission of the European Communities, *General Budget of the European Union for the Fiscal Year 2009*, p. 23.

The EU now obliges third countries to sign 'readmission agreements' as part of overarching partnership accords. These clauses require the partner country to take back expelled workers. But many of these third countries have refused to sign such clauses. Such efforts through common EU-level instruments seem to have overplayed the Union's negotiating hand. In response member states have increasingly pursued their own bilateral migration deals with non-European states. Many member states now link their development aid to readmission agreements.

The EU could certainly be offering more to liberalise visa conditions without ceding completely uncontrolled access to neighbourhood citizens – some concrete benefits of this kind are needed to keep other countries spinning in the EU's orbit. What one would think would be one of the greatest sources of Europe's international power – the incentive of access – has been managed in a way that actually exemplifies everything that is so enervating about its inability to react to decline.

The EU has introduced a number of 'circular mobility schemes', to allow for short-term work contracts in the Union. But these are still relatively limited in scope. The Blue Card scheme introduced in 2009 is voluntary. The EU is trying through new 'mobility partnerships' to correct the brain drain from poorer countries, but developing states are dismissive of these. Circular partnerships are largely symbolic, as they are pertinent only to a limited number of workers, mainly in the agricultural sector. They have done little to assuage developing states' anxieties that the EU is actually making their plight worse in closing off access to unskilled labour while targeting the skilled workers most necessary to poorer nations' growth prospects.

Conclusion

A policy line is emerging in response to Europe's perceived identity crisis: to head off decline, a firmer defence of 'European values' is pursued. This translates into restrictions on migration; forced identity assimilation; surveillance as the principal means of dealing with radicalisation; and the belief that the physical and ideational defensive walls against the Muslim world must be built higher, even though this drains resources and effort from cultivating the economic, social and cultural pastures of Middle Eastern and South-East Asian countries themselves.

All this evokes George Orwell's famous quip that the nationalist spirit is 'power hunger tempered by self-deception'. European governments do indeed deceive themselves in thinking that a kind of Euro-chauvinism represents a viable and enlightened means of dealing with the non-Western world order. It may reflect a predictable hunger to recuperate power and certainty. But it is likely to prove a self-defeating and unviable guiding philosophy.

Europe's identity must stand as cultural pluralism combined with the equanimity of political process. Equanimity, that is, relative to the varying rights claims of different groups. This should be based on a guiding principle that rejects both an arbitrarily engineered 'common identity' on the one hand, and group exceptionalism on the other. This is the identity that will best position Europe to advance economic, political, human rights and security goals in the reshaped world order. Identity that rejects *an* identity. Internal tolerance can become the strongest pillar of a successful external identity. And this must go far beyond the occasional publicity stunt of bringing Islamic leaders from Afghanistan or the Gulf to see 'how well we treat our Muslims'. US security strategy has given a much more positive and prominent role to immigrant communities as a strategic asset than do European policies.

Approaching migration as an existential security threat is either a disingenuous pretext for implementing restrictive policies, or a quite calamitous conflation of what are very different challenges. Dealing with Islamic radicalism cannot be pursued successfully through some kind of identity purification within Europe. The EU must work patiently and carefully to encourage social, economic and political reforms across the Muslim world. Such reforms will not be driven primarily by Western powers. Nor will they provide a magic panacea. Whether or not 'we' engage with Islamists will not be the key determinant in how such movements evolve. But European governments should do what they can to support modernising change. If there is one thing that the non-Western world order will most clearly come to symbolise it is that domestic decisions and structures within the non-West will weigh more heavily on Western interests. For the EU to be executing a series of policies that try to push in precisely the opposite direction is hardly auspicious.

Embedded at the heart of European foreign policy there is a trend towards what we might call culturalism: the attempt to define and extend a particular set of cultural values and identity. But France and other states have it the wrong way round: they support such culturalism but are hesitant over political universalism; what is needed is universalism without the culturalism.

It should be remembered that the EU itself was all about the inclusion of differences at a moment of uncertainty and tension, when it was not clear that those included in the integration project really belonged together or could overcome their differences – intra-European differences, recall, that had produced far more bloodshed than anything so far witnessed in the supposed clash of civilisations.

Liberty cannot be ceded in times of crisis as a trade-off against security or prosperity. Indeed, the link is exactly the opposite of this normally supposed sacrifice. In times of crisis, with so much else at risk, what else is left other than our essential freedoms, individuality and open society? It is more important then than in the boom times when so much else is improving.

5

Citizens' values in a reshaped world

One of the predictions most confidently and frequently proffered is that Europe's decline will leave less scope for a focus on human rights and other 'ethical' dimensions of foreign relations. It is self-evident that the EU faces governments and social movements that today are more buoyant and self-confident in resisting what they insist are 'Western' concepts of individual rights and open politics. And the direction of EU policies reveals that European governments themselves have increasing doubts. Both political will and influence appear to be weakening in European support for human rights and democracy.

A decade ago European states talked confidently of support for human rights being not only ethical but also the best means of safeguarding self-interest. Now diplomats are more likely to talk in familiar terms of a supposed trade-off between normative aspiration and self-interest. And, sceptics assert, even if ethical commitments are retained in principle, Europe's declining influence means that little can now be done to undercut dictators – many of whom head regimes that no longer depend on European largesse or look to Europe for protection or as a role model.

This sense of realism has much to commend it. But, taken too far, it also risks misreading many current trends. Economic decline might be structurally inevitable, but unfavourable trends are less set in stone in the realm of political ideology. The reshaped world order brings with it not only a new balance in state-to-state relations but also sharper demands and potential for popular participation in decision-making in emerging and developing nations.

Democracy certainly faces acute challenges. The incremental expansion in the number of democracies witnessed since the beginning of the 'third wave' of democratisation that commenced in the 1970s has now at least paused, if not ceased. The period 2000–10 was a stagnant decade for democracy, the number of democracies worldwide being no higher in 2010 than in 2000; the first such plateau for four decades. Against such a background, it can seem as if supporting human rights today is akin to trying to push water uphill with a pitchfork. The weakening support for EU positions in the United Nations Human Rights Council – even from some of the biggest recipients of European aid and democracies like South Africa, India and Indonesia – is one of the clearest indications of diminished sway. The evolution of the European integration project has gone hand in hand with the advance of democracy. What now, ask the sceptics, if this is and can no longer be the case?

Notwithstanding the many problems now associated with the political reform agenda, the evidence suggests that among citizens democracy's global spirit remains vibrant. Even where Europe cannot significantly change authoritarian politics in rising powers or developing states, more could and should be done to help empower individual citizens struggling under such regimes. Europe should not feel apologetic about supporting such empowerment as an agenda of universalism. Stepping back from doing so will hasten, rather than temper, Europe's decline. It is understandable that European governments seek a greater sense of control in their relations with foreign powers. But control and political openness are not in opposition with each other. Indeed, the contrary will increasingly be the case – and understanding this will be crucial to navigating the non-Western world.

Despairing drift in EU policies

European support for liberal political values is increasingly oblique. The European Union is moving from being a champion of reform to being a democracy agnostic. Its human rights discourse is akin to peddling snake oil. Talking with government, civil society and business representatives from around the world leaves the distinct impression that, far from being the admirable 'normative power' of academics' imaginings, the EU is increasingly perceived as democracy's dilettante. The EU appears more nonchalant than exercised over democracy's global travails.

The EU's ethical commitments in the field of human rights are, of course, not entirely devoid of substance. But most stress is now placed on the EU doing less, not more; on showing more respect for different political systems, and preaching its own values less; on according greater voice to non-European regimes to set their priorities for the use of European funding. The most strident calls are now for the EU to learn and appreciate political values from other regions, much more than vice versa. The familiar plea now is for the EU to ensure that its support for human rights and democracy entails little more 'interference' than offering information on its own model of region-building.[1] The efforts that the EU does still make to advance democratic values resemble the sporadic lightning strikes of a spent storm.

Endless policy documents and ministerial statements arrive at the same pat conclusion that the EU supports democracy globally simply by offering itself as a model. This is cringingly vainglorious. Lack of knowledge of 'the EU model' is not what is holding back democracy in repressive regimes. Plenty of people in plenty of these regimes know the history of European integration. The EU's experience of post-war reconciliation is undoubtedly impressive and uplifting. But 'teaching' this model does not amount to a policy for defending imperilled human rights around the world.

Anniversary meetings in 2009 of key pro-democracy activists twenty years on from the revolutions in central Europe were uniformly gloomy about Europe's declining commitment to the ideals that spurred democrats in the 1980s and 1990s. The courageous and idealistic central European activists of yesteryear feel like a shrinking band of brothers, not even particularly well connected with the

---

1   International Idea, 'Democracy in development: global consultations on the EU's role in democracy building', Stockholm, 2009.

prevailing cynicism of their own societies.[2] Indeed, support is declining even in the newer member states, democracy's erstwhile champions, for human rights to be prioritised within foreign policy.[3] Something akin to a counter-reformation appears under way. Liberal rights have suffered in countries like Poland and other central European states, and nationalistic tendencies have reared their heads, to the detriment of the newer member states' moral capital in supporting democratic rights within EU foreign policy.

European governments complained constantly during the Bush administration that the abuses carried out by the USA at Guantánamo Bay and Abu Ghraib, as well as through the use of 'extraordinary rendition', undercut efforts to support human rights internationally. They were absolutely correct to do so and to point out that the USA had to get its own house in order before issuing strictures on human rights to the rest of the world. Get Bush out of office, was the message, then we will see more genuine worth in trying to prompt democratisation in the Middle East. Two years on from Bush's departure from office, President Obama has admirably cleaned up the USA's own act, but this has not spurred Europeans into their promised action. Europe has reneged on its side of an implicit transatlantic understanding.

In early 2010 the EU agreed an Agenda for Action to guide

---

2   Conference 'Return to Europe: reflections after 20 years of democratic renewal', organised by PASOS, Prague, 9/10 December 2009.

3   Zora Bútorová and Olga Gyarfásová, 'Return to Europe: new freedoms embraced, but weak public support for assisting democracy further afield', Policy Brief, PASOS, Prague, 2009.

its human rights and democracy policies. This does finally provide a common framework and set of principles for European policies. But it remains an extremely low-key initiative that even most officials in Brussels and national capitals have not heard of. The Agenda offers no new resources or means of pressure. Indeed, it states that political conditionality is not the way forward – this after many member states initially opposed the new strategy on the grounds that it might lead to additional pressure on dictators.[4]

All member states are apparently content that the new Agenda for Action constitutes a radical step forward, even though it is so patently anodyne. It gives the impression that all that is needed for more effective human rights support is a set of streamlined institutions, and a reshuffling of diplomats from the Commission, Council and member states to the External Action Service. Much is made of the EAS's potential. But this will be structured in almost the same way as the Commission's external relations department (Relex) which preceded its creation. The proposed structure for the EAS currently has nine geographical directorate-generals and only one catch-all thematic directorate-general which includes human rights at a relatively low level of priority. The European Parliament has launched a campaign criticising the absence of a higher-level human rights department in the EAS. The current Relex has one person engaged in democracy promotion full time – compare this to the massive expansion of CSDP military staff and one has an illustration

---

4   Council of the European Union, 'Council conclusions on democracy support in the EU's external relations', 2974th External Relations Council meeting, European Council, Brussels, 17 November 2009.

of how the EU cannot be seen as such a soft, progressive liberal power. The EAS might be described as a Relex redux: a different set of diplomats but undertaking the same type of function, organised around traditional government-to-government relations. A boost for human rights around the world it most certainly is not.

Authoritarian powers around the world are now much more critical of the EU than the EU is of them. The standard critical line now runs that European states obsess over elections as an inappropriately Western-specific measure of democracy. This is simply not the case. Just a selection of examples from the immediate neighbourhood in recent years, of stolen elections that failed to elicit any substantively critical European response, and were even followed by upgrades in EU relations, includes: Armenia in 2008, Kazakhstan in 2007, Egypt in 2005, Morocco in 2007 and Tunisia in 2009. European Parliament election observers complain that they even get leant on by EU governments to give unfree elections a clean bill of health. And they express anger at member-state diplomats rubbishing MEPs' critical comments – in the words of one observer, 'stabbing us in the back'.

New agreements signed or offered to countries that are highly autocratic and even becoming more so include those to Syria, Libya, Turkmenistan, the southern Caucasus states, Vietnam, Singapore and Zimbabwe. With 10,000 Russian soldiers still on its territory, Georgia had explicitly asked the EU not to resume talks with Moscow – it did so. A new EU–Russia Partnership for Modernisation agreed in mid-2010 completely sidelines human rights. Many new regional agreements – such as the 2007 EU–Central Asia Strategy – have watered down language on democracy and human rights. This has led to fears that they may undermine the 'essential elements' clauses that are designed to give such rights commitments some bite within pre-existing bilateral accords. There is now a rumbling debate in Brussels over the possible removal of such clauses.

No single EU exports control agency exists to temper member states' tendency to undercut each other in a race to boost sales to autocratic regimes. Caution reigns even in the use of sanctions narrowly targeted at regime officials responsible for the most egregious of human rights abuses.[5] Following pressure from Germany, the EU was even unable to retain sanctions on Uzbekistan, where the Karimov regime excels at boiling political opponents alive and gunning down peaceful protests. In Uzbekistan, the EU even lifted an arms embargo, a visa ban on top officials and a demand for an inquiry into the notorious 2005 Andijan massacre at which government troops killed 500 people. The EU was not asking for wholesale democratisation but simply an investigation into this horrendous event – and yet even this effort proved too much principle for most European governments.

Policy betrays a growing European preference for only partial political change – a slight diminution of repression, without efforts that might endanger the power of autocratic regimes. This is summarised evocatively by one Kazakh

---

5   Council of the European Union, 'Guidelines on implementation and evaluation of restrictive measures (sanctions) in the framework of the EU common foreign and security policy', 17464/09, General Secretariat of the Council, Brussels, 15 December 2009.

democrat, thrown into jail in 2010 without a European response, who judges the international community thus: 'Before I was forced to say that 2 + 2 = 12; now I can say 2 + 2 = 5; but you will still not push for me to be able to answer 4.'

The case of a Western Saharan activist who was expelled from Morocco to Spain and went on hunger strike at the end of 2009 placed European impotence on display. The Spanish and French governments refused to criticise the Moroccan regime for the expulsion. Europe had to wait for US mediation. In return for Morocco accepting the repatriation of the activist, language was agreed that strengthened Morocco's position on the Western Saharan dispute in contravention of an ongoing UN process.

This case was humiliating for Spain, but it was in line with its recent drift in foreign policy. Indeed, in Spain, they talk of the 'Zapatero paradox': the prime minister's avowedly progressive focus on rights and gender issues within Spain abruptly stops at the country's border. In recent years, the Spanish government has pursued bilateral strategic partnerships with the likes of Russia and China, quite clearly abrogating common EU language on human rights and democracy. Spain still gives over half its human rights funding to Latin America, leaving little for reformers in non-democratic states.

Critics complain that punitive measures target weaker and strategically marginal African states when they are eschewed elsewhere. This imbalance is indeed a pernicious element of EU policy. But even in Africa the EU can hardly be accused of being overly zealous in its pressure for democratic reform. The EU invariably opens a formal dialogue with those African countries judged to be seriously infringing human rights – as it is legally obliged to do under the Cotonou accords – but then allows talks to drag on for many months even as further atrocities take place. This has happened recently in Guinea. The EU opened consultations to express its concern after a military coup in December 2008; very light sanctions were imposed only after an army massacre against protesters almost a year later in September 2009. An arms embargo now imposed on Guinea is largely symbolic as the country gets most of its weapons from the immediate region, not Europe. In 2009 in Niger and Madagascar similar responses meant that development aid already committed continued, with only new projects held in abeyance.

And there are many, many more cases of sanctions not being imposed. There are numerous examples of states receiving handsome increases in European aid and/or diplomatic partnership as their political and civic rights deteriorate. In recent years, such examples include Ethiopia, Eritrea, Uganda, Kenya, Ivory Coast, Gabon, Chad, the Central African Republic, Togo, Equatorial Guinea and Rwanda. Even in Zimbabwe, where sanctions have been imposed, the European Commission has broadened out the scope of its humanitarian aid so as to undertake traditional development support. Measures adopted unilaterally by member states – such as Sweden's reduction of aid to Uganda in 2010 – are infrequent. African civic leaders criticise the EU's tendency to support stability-oriented power-sharing deals that in effect allow autocrats to get away with rigging elections for the modest price of allowing opposition forces a small stake in government.

There are of course genuinely difficult policy consid-erations to bear in mind. In cases such as Belarus, the EU has tried a policy of ostracism, to little avail. In such cases a modest swing towards engagement is justified, at least to gain an initial foothold from which pressure can be subse-quently brought to bear. In Belarus, however, the evidence suggests that this engagement is already being oriented towards security aims – the countering of Russian influ-ence – rather than used as a toehold for efforts to push for at least a degree of political reform. Sanctions on Belarus were waived again in early 2010 at the very same moment that the regime was arresting 40 civic activists.

Burma is a similar case. Big divisions exist on policy towards Burma. A majority of member states now want an easing of sanctions. A retention of sanctions is supported by only a small minority of states (the UK, the Czech Republic, the Netherlands, Ireland and Denmark). Pleas by the main opposition National League for Democracy party for stiffer sanctions have gone unheeded. It is widely perceived that the EU has relaxed its position on Burma because of the growing importance of unblocking relations with ASEAN.

The influential Responsibility to Protect (R2P) concept has been a double-edged sword for human rights: it has boosted the focus on the need to respond to the very worst mass atrocities in conflict situations, but at the cost of shifting attention and resources away from the less dramatic cases of rights infringements. Moreover, one European prime-ministerial adviser argues that even the relatively 'sexy' R2P concept cannot today be sold to European publics in the midst of economic crisis.

Politicians constantly say Europe is distinguished by its human rights record and prioritises this as part of its foreign policy. Many individual cases show it isn't and it doesn't. To give just one typical instance: in spring 2010 a Jordanian woman, whose NGO had received EU funds, was put on trial by her government simply for advocating stronger human rights protection. At that very moment, the EU was updating a paper on supporting human rights defenders. Despite this, EU ambassadors decided not to intervene in her protection. One wonders how much such victims feel comforted by Europe's sanctimonious talk of its unique human rights identity.

European donors do provide funding for human rights and democracy initiatives across the world. This is seen as a preferable route to coercive diplomatic pressure. While the amounts offered for such 'political aid' have increased, they are still modest relative to the scale of challenges involved. And under this label of democracy assistance, most European donors opt for relatively safe projects. Rather than backing dissidents they offer technical aid to ministries to improve formal human rights legislation. Rather than fostering genuinely independent voices among the business sector, they boost civil service capacity to design better economic policy. Rather than keep opposition forces functioning they fund bridge-building dialogues. This author has heard many European policymakers advocating a retreat even from supporting basic freedom of expression projects, on the grounds of these being perceived as unduly 'Western'. One African complains that all this represents, on the part of European development agencies, a 'wilful and complicit misunderstanding of the principle of ownership', taken to mean 'ownership of aid funds by regimes, not populations'.

Member states' democracy and human rights funding initiatives generally lack critical bite. France has reduced its human rights budget since 2006 and continues to have a very state-oriented focus in its external support programmes. In contrast, 20 per cent of overall Swedish aid goes to civil society; Sweden has also restarted democracy programmes in Russia. Germany works in particular on decentralisation. The UK and the Netherlands have linked democracy aid more to security and fragile state concerns. Denmark is now launching an independent institution for political party support. So, the trends are mixed. Amounts of funding are not negligible but tend to mix democracy with other aims, such as social cohesion, so that it is difficult to be sure that most of these resources are really being spent in a way that enhances political liberalisation.[6]

It is self-evident that the EU now exerts little critical diplomatic pressure on China. On the issues of Tibet, Taiwan, Hong Kong, repression against the Uighur Muslim minority and political prisoner cases, the EU has fallen into line and does little more than mumble homilies largely for its own domestic audience. All member states now formally recognise Chinese sovereignty over Tibet. After some very public spats between the UK and France, Spain and Germany, the EU retains an arms embargo on China; but this has not prevented increases in military sales to the People's Republic. Indeed, the arms embargo is in fact weaker than more

---

6   FRIDE, *Factsheets on Democracy Support*, available at www.fride.org.

general EU positions on arms sales. China has cancelled summits and meetings with European governments and the EU collectively with impunity. This European caution is despite the fact that when a member state has previously spoken out on a particular human rights case there is little evidence that the Chinese have commercially punished that country.[7]

Perhaps less acknowledged is the fact that even at a lower, less politicised level European efforts to support reform in China are weakening. Support for village elections was forthcoming from several European donors for a number of years in the early 2000s but has now been discontinued. Legal reform initiatives are funded, for example under an EU–China Legal and Judicial Cooperation Programme, but limit themselves to the issues of commercial law that directly interest European investors. The Charter 08 democratic movement demonstrates growing demand for open politics, with which European governments have not engaged. China has prevented a number of critical NGOs, even on the European side, from being involved in human rights dialogue.

Europeans are comforted that President Obama's vision on spreading democracy sounds just like Europe's: no imposition, a link being made between political reform and social justice, more funds going through governments than through civic opposition movements. Obama is the first president who does not instinctively believe that the USA

---

7   House of Lords, European Union Committee, 'Stars and dragons: the EU and China', 7th Report of Session 2009–10, House of Lords, London, March 2010, p. 20.

can transform the world. The USA has criticised Russia and China on human rights, however, while offsetting this with efforts to reset overarching strategic relations. Chinese control of the Internet has jolted the USA into more of a focus on political rights, far more so than Europeans. For all his caution, Obama has pumped up reform-oriented aid budgets, such as the Millennium Challenge Account and Middle East Partnership Initiative.[8] Much is written about Obama's lukewarm commitment to human rights and democracy around the world; but far from filling the vacuum this creates, the EU is still lumbering behind.

European governments have slipped too comfortably into an attitude of passive idealism. They commonly argue that external support for democracy must await the right moment, in the long term; but they do nothing to make the arrival of that 'right moment' more likely. This position is akin to saying little more than if democracy comes we will back it, if not we'll stay perched on our fence. The nominally progressive sceptics have provided a respectable cloak of strategic convenience. Many diplomats throw up their hands: of course we support human rights and democracy, they proclaim, but we can best help by staying out of countries' internal politics; are we not told now, in the name of morality, to be careful about foisting 'our' values on to other societies, anyway? So let us just carry on with our traditional diplomacy in the meantime …

But there is no position of absolute neutrality. Europe

8   Stephen McInerney, 'The federal budget and appropriations for fiscal year 2010: democracy, governance and human rights in the Middle East', PoMed, Washington, DC, 2010.

is sufficiently intertwined with most regions around the world that it unavoidably has influence, in a direction that makes democracy either more or less likely. When the EU gives the Egyptian government 300 million euros, no one complains about intervention in local politics. When it gives a civil society organisation 20,000 euros, cries of neo-imperialism ring out. Yet the former loads the dice far more firmly against democracy than the latter grant does in reform's favour. Europe seemed less afraid to plough its human rights furrow in the past than it is today: during the Cold War the Federal Republic of Germany provided vital credit to the neighbouring Democratic Republic specifically in return for rights improvements. Today the EU does not even meet the minimalist yardstick of 'doing no harm' to democracy's prospects.

The putrefied carrot of enlargement

Of course, it is rightfully said that, whatever the limits to Europe's global efforts, on its own immediate periphery the EU has played a major role in spurring democratic reform. While this is undoubtedly true, there are also signs that the power of EU enlargement as a democracy promotion tool is weakening. The carrot of enlargement is turning sour. The Euro-sphere is becoming a Euro-buffer, a no man's land of political indeterminacy.

The enlargement process now seems designed to hold aspirant countries in a condition of 'neither-nor'. The EU wishes to avoid both the strategic fall-out of definitively rejecting countries *and* the domestic costs of extending membership farther outward. Candidates and potential candidates are deliberately held in a holding pattern, with fading prospects of ever touching down in Euro-land.

As is well known, accession negotiations with Turkey are well and truly stuck. Cyprus is the big barrier. From a Turkish perspective, the EU has failed to keep its promises to open direct trade and aid programmes with northern Cyprus. Meanwhile, Turkey's democratic reform process is in the balance. The Erdogan government has intervened against independently minded judges and journalists. The army once again stands closer guard over secular constitutional values. In 2009 a key Kurdish party was shut down. A harsh Commission report in October 2009 criticised deliberalisation measures in Turkey. Scores of 'Have we lost Turkey?' round tables are now held across Europe. Ruling AKP party spokesmen say they have completely lost patience with the EU; the latter's presence in Turkish domestic political debate has almost disappeared.

In 2010 Turkey briefly withdrew its ambassador from Sweden in response to a parliamentary debate over the Armenian 'genocide' – a sign of a new, unnecessary but symbolic belligerence towards even Turkey's traditional 'friends' within the European Union. The EU is not even doing much to help Turkey other than through the accession process. No broader security agreement has been offered. Nor has an accord with the European Defence Agency, such as fellow non-EU NATO member Norway enjoys. Slightly bizarrely, Turkey itself now doles out more aid to other countries than it receives from the European Union. Its visa accords with Russia and several Arab states have given it more concrete benefits than what is on offer from the EU in terms of freedom of movement. While the EU's message to the former Soviet states of central Europe in the 1990s was 'You are part of the family, you will be part of Europe', to Turkey it is still 'Reform, then we'll see'.

In the Balkans, it appears more likely that promises of EU membership will – eventually – be followed through. This region may well represent enlargement's last hurrah. But the road to democracy is proving rocky. The EU has undertaken some brave and principled interventions in the Balkans in recent years. In 2008 the EU risked its hand and played a role in getting moderate, reformist president Boris Tadic elected in Serbia, by quite clearly linking the signing of a new agreement to his election.

But serious shortcomings in EU policy persist. An extra condition has been added that the EU's 'absorption capacity' must be sufficient for future enlargements to proceed. This ill-defined prerequisite is interpreted in the Balkans as an all-purpose blocking device. Angela Merkel has wondered aloud whether the Balkans (beyond Croatia) should fall into the same category as Turkey and be deserving of only a 'privileged partnership'.

Moreover, the Balkans receives only a fraction of the per capita aid amounts that central and eastern European states enjoyed to help smooth their path into the Union. And democracy aid channelled to the region has taken a nosedive in the last five years. Visa liberalisation offered to Balkan states has been made conditional on their strengthening border controls, not on democratic reform. Cross-border crime is now the big concern in the Balkans; criminal networks still enjoy political patronage which the pre-accession process does not appear to be dislodging. New enlargement commissioner Stefan Füle admits: 'we have let the pre-accession process become too technical because it no longer occupies the forefront of our minds'.[9]

Even in the Balkan candidate countries, the Union has struggled to make sure that regimes abide by the technical EU governance standards they have signed on to their books. Here 'democratic governance' aid in practice aims at helping states adopt the body of existing EU laws and policies (or *acquis*), not necessarily more democratic decision-making. Indeed, money from the Commission's Instrument for Pre-Accession focusing on implementation of the *acquis* has been demonstrably proven not to be synonymous with deepening political reform.[10] One Albanian civic activist puts it well: in focusing on a series of very formal and technical governance rules, the EU plays along with a 'culture of no implementation'.

In the Balkans, ostensibly democracy-related conditionality has become a tool of strategic calculus. The EU's group of 'friends of the Balkans' increasingly insists that conditions should be toned down to get countries from the region admitted as soon as possible. These governments have sought to push back political reform requirements to the very end of the enlargement process.

The sceptical member states, ironically including those

---

9   Stefan Füle, speech at the Brussels Forum, Brussels, 26–28 March 2010.

10 Judy Batt, 'Signs of hope in the Western Balkans?', FRIDE Policy Brief, Fundación para las Relaciones Internacionales y el Diálogo Exterior, Madrid, November 2009.

most hostile to assertive democracy promotion in most regions of the world, are now the purists that insist on strict political compliance – which conveniently pushes back enlargement. The EU lets brutally repressed elections in the Arab world and Asia go uncensored, but concerns itself with the far subtler electoral misdeeds of Balkan states, compounding the impression that pressing for democratic perfection has become a pretext for delaying difficult decisions on enlargement. One good example was the Albanian election in 2009.

A majority of member states adhere to a 'Serbia first' position in the Balkans. They argue that Serbia's strategic centrality to the region means that conditions should be relaxed to get this state into the EU as quickly as possible. Serbia's pre-accession agreement with the Union was reluctantly unblocked late in 2009 by the Netherlands – although its final ratification may still depend on Belgrade delivering key war crimes suspects to the international tribunal in The Hague.

Even members of the current reformist Serb government insist that they will never accept Kosovo's independence, which would scupper any prospect of Serbia joining the Union. Its ministers have often insisted that if Serbia has to choose between Kosovo and Europe it will not opt for the latter. With five EU members themselves refusing to recognise Kosovo, it is not surprising that the Union has so far failed to persuade Serbia to relent on this question. Even if a compromise deal on Kosovo eventually emerges (as Tadic himself has intimated is possible), the EU's confusion on this issue has already vastly compromised its influence over democratic reforms.

The five EU member states that refuse to recognise Kosovo have delayed a pre-accession agreement with Pristina. Far from helping the new state, Spain is even blocking Kosovo's eligibility for European Bank for Reconstruction and Development loans. The EULEX rule-of-law mission is not operating in the north of Kosovo, engendering fears that the EU is being too indulgent in ceding autonomous status to Serb areas in Kosovo in a way that will open a Pandora's box of claims across the region.

Relations with Bosnia proceed in halting fashion, with the EU constantly delaying the deepening of majoritarian democracy as nationalist leaders cling to the precarious ethnic power-sharing deal that ended the civil war in 1995. EU efforts to resurrect the issue of constitutional reform in late 2009 were too half-hearted to force a breakthrough. In addition, strongly reforming Macedonia has been rebuffed by a Greek veto, wielded on the apparently tangential issue of the country's name – Macedonia's Ohrid peace agreement is now unravelling in part as a result of this uncertain context. Accession talks with Montenegro have also been pushed back. In sum, the EU is doing very much less than it might be doing to encourage democratic deepening in the still-brittle Balkans.

Since 2009 the EU has been running an Eastern Partnership with Ukraine, Belarus, Moldova and the three southern Caucasus states. This offers modest increases in aid, trade access, technical cooperation and some visa liberalisation. Whether it is designed to prioritise support for human rights and democracy is still not clear. Analyst Nicu Popescu argues perceptively that the logic behind deeper EU engagement in its eastern neighbourhood is increasingly one of old-fashioned strategic counterbalancing of Russia.

This has patently been the case in Georgia, where the almost jingoistically pro-Western Mikhail Saakashivili has been supported even as he has centralised power and dragged the country away from democratic consolidation. Breaking all the best practice of democracy-building, European governments even paid the salaries of the president's immediate team from funds that had previously been destined for civil society. Russia and Turkey are intensifying their own southern Caucasus initiatives, in some areas – such as help in overcoming the financial crisis – offering juicier and more immediately edible carrots than the European Union. EU–Russia competition in this region is increasingly that between spheres of influence rather than democratic versus non-democratic strategies.

Ukraine is perhaps the most glaring case where EU carrots have failed to get the digestive juices pumping. Six years on from the Orange Revolution Ukraine has not been granted the offer of EU membership that so openly motivated the democrats who took to the streets to oust the kleptocratic Kuchma regime. The EU has offered free trade, technical cooperation, defence assistance and many other lesser-order goodies. Indeed, its range of new initiatives in Ukraine shows much admirable creativity. But the thing Ukraine most wants – as even the country's friends in the EU, such as Poland, admit – is today a more distant prospect than one might have imagined in 2004.

Germany and a handful of other member states would not even allow Ukraine to define itself as 'European' in its new agreement with the Union, for fear that this would recognise its right to candidacy. The EU's message to Ukraine is to forget membership and concentrate on 'getting its own house in order'. But European aid to help the country in its reforms is less than one fifth the amount that Turkey receives.

In February 2010, Ukrainians voted back into office Viktor Yanukovich, the pro-Russian strongman who had been defeated in the Orange Revolution. Some observers argue this provides a positive opportunity for the EU to renew its influence over Ukraine, by demonstrating that its strategy is pro-democracy rather than anti-Russian. This may prove to be the case. But note this opinion from a Ukrainian journalist: Yanukovich's victory may be good for Ukrainian democracy but almost in the perverse sense of it revealing the frustration with constantly looking to the EU for solutions. Shortly after the 2010 elections, Ukraine signed a deal extending Russia's right to station its Black Sea fleet at Sebastopol in return for a deal on cheap gas and an injection of Russian infrastructure funding. Ukrainian officials insist that the gas deal has done more to head off financial insolvency than anything on the table from the European Union. Yanukovich is narrowing democratic freedoms, even as he takes forward practical cooperation on incorporating EU economic regulations more than his predecessor.

The case of Ukraine appears to represent the end of enlargement being deployed as security strategy: most member states now will do anything not to annoy Russia by suggesting that Ukrainian accession might have a strategic dimension to it. Ukraine's stalled democratisation must stand as one of the most disappointing indictments of European normative influence in recent years. Nowhere more than in Ukraine has the EU seemed to partake in tugging defeat from the jaws of victory.

Wrap all these cases together and it is clear that today a really difficult question is asked of the Union: during the last three decades a good dose of European power has flowed from the EU deliberately not setting limits to its borders; so what happens when such constructive ambivalence trips over its own elusive shadow?

Optimists might say that the *possibility* of accession is what counts, more than its actual granting. Accession is the mirage dragging expectant states though the desert of costly reforms. Has it not already played its part in Ukraine and Turkey? Turkey today is broadly democratic, open and prosperous economically, and has (some would say) less radical Islam than the north of England. The official EU line on Turkey's new assertive foreign policy is positive. Some analysts say that Europe is not so much 'losing Turkey' as benefiting from the latter's more independent diplomacy in Syria, Iran and the Occupied Territories.

But such sanguinity would be too optimistic. Basic political psychology kicks in: your influence must suffer more if your break your promises than if you had never made those promises in the first place. And this has concrete policy implications. While Turkey's new diplomacy has to date undoubtedly been welcome, it must be the case that Turkish EU membership would reduce the risk of the country's post-Kemalist foreign policy drifting off in more problematic, neo-Ottoman directions. Some analysts say Turkey actually fears cooperating too much with European governments on broader international questions because such pragmatic partnership might be taken as a substitute for accession. Keeping states in suspended orbit must eventually tax the EU's creative diplomacy: if gravity does not pull these countries inward, the likelihood is that they will break loose and embark on a more distant trajectory.

Beyond state resistance

There needs to be engagement with non-democratic regimes and flexibility over different political models. But the EU's baleful obsequiousness to dictators goes way beyond this. Engagement with autocrats is necessary and proper. Debasing deference is not. Europeans should listen to the grievances and value-claims of other powers; but not with such convenient naivety. In many cases supporting human rights is merely a question of holding non-democratic governments to commitments they have happily signed up to in international bodies.

Preserving influence in a reshaped world is *not* only a matter of ingratiating the Chinese leadership. It will be conditioned by the way in which different powers relate to citizens' aspirations. Where the EU should aim to edify, it leaves citizens increasingly adrift. The EU should aim not merely to conciliate but to inspire and empower. Can the idealistic activists of other countries not themselves revitalise the normative orientation of a Europe sliding into materialistic saturation and apathy?

It is commonly argued that support for human rights and democracy has often not worked because it is insufficiently 'demand-led'. This poses the questions of how much demand for such support really exists within non- or semi-democratic states around the world. At FRIDE we assembled a team of researchers to undertake a project designed to assess precisely this question: what do civil society organisations within target countries think about the democracy support agenda?

Our team of researchers conducted nearly six hundred interviews across fifteen countries, with a range of local 'stakeholders', including civic leaders, political party cadres and government representatives. We compiled information on their judgements of why democracy support is not working as well as might be the case, and their views on how donors' strategies must adapt.

The results of our project reveal the profound disappointment that exists with the tepidness of European (and other Western) support. Local stakeholders do not want donors to give up the ghost. The most potent complaint was over the scarcity of democracy assistance resources, not their surfeit. Despite all the difficulties of recent years, and erstwhile 'overstretch' of some Western governments' democracy support policies, there is patent demand for help from outside.

People from across different regions react angrily when Western governments and experts claim there is no 'local demand' for political reform, which local stakeholders feel is invariably a pretext for inaction. The view that Western powers are foisting democracy on ambivalent societies is simply not borne out by research. Solidarity in democracy support among southern NGOs is growing, says one African civil society representative, just as the EU is stepping back from supporting them. Unlike the USA and Australia,

Europe is withdrawing democracy aid in Indonesia, when the latter's government is seeking more assistance in strengthening democratic institutions. Indonesian diplomats complain that they have received little firm support from the EU for their efforts to push the democracy agenda within ASEAN, for example through the Bali Democracy Forum. When a number of developing countries asked for democracy to be included as a ninth Millennium Development Goal, European governments opposed this plea.

Local stakeholders want European governments to be less risk averse. They want external democracy promoters to be prepared to take risks sometimes, even if mistakes are made. Their general feeling is that most funders now 'play it too safe'. The judgement is that, as regimes have become smarter at neutralising political aid, the international community has reacted by withdrawing into a shell of insipidness rather than showing a willingness to experiment and be more ambitious in its funding structures. Europe increasingly plays along with the way that state actions ossify political and social structures.

To paraphrase one civil society activist: locals are not necessarily waiting around for the international community to show 'respect' for the 'shared values' of whichever autocratic regime. We picked up much concern that such well-meaning guiding maxims can end up seeming rather hollow in the eyes of harassed and persecuted civil society organisations in target states. NGOs in non-European states often say that they wish that more active member states would break ranks with the EU so as not to be held back by those most reticent to offer support.

A crucial and more political observation was made by a large number of our interviewees: much more valuable than slightly increased amounts of money, or slightly changed funding rules, would be more effective international pressure on regimes to loosen civil society and other laws. There is now enough accumulated experience to suggest that, without such changes, funding a small number of human rights projects invariably has relatively limited potential. Local stakeholders are, almost without exception, looking for a much tighter linkage between project funding and the nature of diplomatic relations between donor governments and non-democratic regimes. The lack of such a connection is almost universally seen as a major cause of democracy assistance's increasingly disappointing record. It is seen as of little value to fund stand-alone democracy projects if the issue of political reform does not permeate the full panoply of foreign policy instruments – trade, energy, development. The need is to move beyond a donor–recipient relation: economically empowered people around the world are looking not for aid but for international diplomatic support for political rights.

Conclusions

The EU is failing to follow Aung San Suu Kyi's famous injunction: to use its freedom to advance that of others. What is the European attitude towards dictators today? Germany genuflects. France fawns. Spain surrenders. Italy ingratiates. Others muddle through with ineffectual uncertainty. To criticise Europe's softness on human rights and democracy is not to advocate swingeing punitive tactics. Liberal theorists are right to caution that completely ostracising 'rogue' states from the international community can end up merely castigating blameless citizens and striking an anti-cosmopolitan note.[11] But there must be a proper mid-point between imposing comprehensive sanctions and spineless appeasement.

Compounding the dearth of political will, doubt increasingly exists that Europe has the power to make much difference to the course of politics outside its borders. When history no longer seems to be moving quite so definitively in democracy's direction (if it ever was), the costs of pushing for liberal politics appear all the more prohibitive. Combine the paucity of will and lack of capacity, and according priority to democracy in foreign policy can seem increasingly inadvisable. We come close to venerating a nullity in constantly claiming the EU's moral superiority as a diligent defender of democracy.

The EU still feels relatively confident in espousing the universalism of a limited number of core human rights. The use of torture and the death penalty are easily condemned as obviously 'bad things'. But the same confidence evaporates when it comes to broader political rights. European states feel more at ease in supporting civic rights than 'political freedom'. The latter language is widely rejected among European diplomats as specifically 'American'. In fact, European liberals were arguing as far back as the eighteenth century that civil liberties are fragile in the absence

---

11 The view of John Rawls, as cited in Robert Fine, *Cosmopolitanism*, Routledge, London, 2007.

of political liberty.[12] Whatever the justified concerns over the tone of some US policies, it is to the EU's discredit that this early observation has been neglected.

To presume that the tide now pushes definitively against democracy is to misread social trends and aspirations around the world. Supporting democracy can be a means of preserving Europe's standing in the world and of anticipating the empowering dynamism that economic modernisation and technological change can (although do not always) bring in their wake.

This means that European support for democratic rights must take its cue from citizens. Elites may have won the battle in pushing back Western support for democracy, but this does not mean that they have done a service to their citizens. A focus on citizens' rights would be more propitious than promoting democracy through the lingering prism of the Cold War. The language of the 'free world' defending democracy as a bulwark against communism no longer resonates with today's younger populations. But, in respect of such a citizen-led logic, European governments are cautious because they today frequently raise questions about whether democracy and liberal human rights are really 'authentic' to societies outside Europe. A growing ambivalence on this question today constitutes a major impediment to the EU addressing the concerns of local stakeholders.

John Keane's majestic history of democracy offers some good grounds for rejecting fashionable relativism. He shows that the roots of democracy emerged in several non-Western

---

12 Wilson, op. cit., p. 113.

areas. Local activists in India do not accept sceptical academics' view that poor countries 'need to be fit before democracy', and argue instead that they 'need to become fit through democracy'. India has already knocked on the head the idea that democracy leaves no room for traditional values.[13] Several South-East Asian states, such as Indonesia, are increasingly supporting democratic norms at a regional level and yet the EU has done nothing to harness this change in attitude.

It is absolutely right to be flexible and attentive to the danger of foisting alien institutions on other societies. But the issue should not be the 'authentic' per se. The trend in policy that extols the 'traditional' is not without serious pitfalls. Apart from anything else, uncritically reifying the 'authentic' ignores the fact that everything is at some stage introduced to a particular society and thus at that moment is not authentic. Rather, the challenge is to make such forms as have local support more democratic. Rather than these being seen to rest on a spurious village/community/tribal/religious/national unity of voice, they can and should be used as the basis for greater plurality and freedom of expression. It is worth recalling Niall Ferguson's point that the essence of British imperialism was support for traditional structures – support that was ultimately part of its fall, as it engendered resistance from modernising forces.[14]

Rejection of neo-imperialism does not entail rejection

---

13 John Keane, *The Life and Death of Democracy*, Simon and Schuster, London, 2009, pp. 571 and 586.
14 Niall Ferguson, *Empire: How Britain Made the Modern World*, Penguin, London, 2004, p. 210.

of support for liberal democratic values. In this sense, Europe's ultra-caution is unwarranted and is not progressive: the potential for democratic reform is latent, not exogenous. It merits renewed European sponsorship. Weakening European support for human rights and democracy is one of the most dispiriting dimensions of Europe's fall.

6
The chimera of a European economy

Before the financial crisis struck in autumn 2008, Europe was already sliding down a path of relative economic decline. The crisis has transformed background unease over long-term trends into panic over the prospect of precipitous collapse. In 2010 the concern has been with simply preventing the eurozone from unravelling, not long-term strategy to temper international decline. As this book goes to press, the danger of such internal fracturing appears to have lessened. But there are still many who think that, far from being able to articulate a coherent policy for mitigating decline, the EU may very soon exist only in highly diluted form.

Our concern here is to assess how management of the current economic crisis relates to the EU's underlying role in and influence over the global economy. The basic dilemma is well known. Growth rates in rising powers have exceeded those in Europe. Many such powers are flush with funds that accord them new leverage over European economies – although they now also face difficulties by virtue of being tied into the toxic assets of debtor countries. Europe struggles to retain competitiveness. The importance of avoiding a slide into protectionism is frequently emphasised. Public debt run up during the financial crisis will hang heavily around the European financial neck for many years.

The crisis has gone through two phases: a banking sector crisis has led into a sovereign debt crisis. In the first, the response was regulation. In the second, Germany has pushed a response focused on fiscal stringency. Neither response has prioritised structural reform aimed at enhancing long-term growth. The way in which European governments have scrambled to save the euro and a modicum of internal economic solidarity has done little to address the underlying challenges of international political economy.

Beyond the short-term imperatives of crisis management, the fundamental question of how the European Union relates structurally to the world economy must be addressed. In this sense, the signs are that EU policy favours strengthening the exclusivity of the European economy. The model is one of a tighter regional bloc competing against other regional blocs in a rebalanced world system. The financial crisis has hastened what were already incipient moves in this direction.

This is the wrong way to manage decline. What is needed is exactly the opposite: less focus on a preferential distinction between the European and global economies. The increasing resort to boosting national or European champions is the wrong way forward. Nor is the EU right in its increasing fondness for picking off individual powers with whom to negotiate economic deals on a bilateral basis. Such deals focus on highly selective and instrumental trade and investment aims, pushed on to other states in return for ad hoc political trade-offs. They do not reflect a well-thought-out set of principles for managing economic decline. Grappling with such decline is not about defending an illusory and supposedly unique European model against the vicissitudes of the world beyond. Rather, it should be about a more flexible and agile harnessing of global change to fashion new ways of meeting material aspirations.

Model or mirage?
The optimists still contend that Europe's social market economic model puts it ahead of the game. They insist that its combination of market efficiency and state provisions will enable it to turn back the tide of competition from emerging powers. This school of thought argues that the latter's rise has been overhyped when most rising economies remain internally brittle and still languish far behind Europe on all qualitative criteria of economic success. They also argue that, looking beyond the immediate problems with the euro, the EU is actually better positioned in exiting the financial crisis than other powers, and that this crisis in fact vindicates more than it weakens Europe's economic model. The type of government-guided fostering of employment and industry that distinguishes the 'European model' is just what is back in vogue, it is contended, and what is likely to stand Europe in good stead in future decades. The optimists argue that EU economies already incorporate the kind of automatic stabilisers rendered so much more necessary by the crisis. Some say that many European countries moved quickly to regulate banks when the crisis struck, and this was widely seen as crucial to stemming the depth of financial collapse.

Some analysts contend that, contrary to the perception of

European rigidity, much progress has already been made on 'flexicurity' – the notion of protecting not particular jobs but the individual worker through different cycles of employment. European governments have certainly pumped increasing amounts of funds into preparing workers for newly competitive sectors through such 'flexicurity' programmes. European Union protection for temporary workers was extended in 2008 – clearly a good thing, and beneficial to employee motivation, skill-building and productivity. Optimists also argue that the demographic time bomb is not as serious as is routinely suggested: while pensioners are increasing in number, the number of children per family is reducing so that the overall share of non-working dependants is not set to increase that much. Moreover, most member states are already moving to raise the retirement age.[1]

In bald figures there is much to comfort Europeans. The EU remains by far the largest investor in most markets around the world. Its multinationals are prospering and enjoy a healthy (if diminishing) presence in rankings of top global companies. China's development has offered up a lucrative market of which European firms have taken great advantage. It is ironic that as France frets at length about what globalisation does to *it*, huge Carrefour stores blot the skyline of many a Third World mega-city. For the moment the USA still has more direct investment stock in Spain than in China and India combined. The despair that comes from extrapolating current emerging-power growth rates far into

---

1 A particularly egregious recent example of such optimism is Steven Hill, *Europe's Promise*, University of California Press, Berkeley, CA, 2010.

the future overlooks the fact that these countries will hit problems as they enter more mature phases of economic development. Abiding European economic power is demonstrated by a string of cases in which the EU has successfully taken on American corporate might – as, for example, when in May 2009 the Commission fined Intel $1.5 billion.

It is certainly true that much doomsaying is exaggerated – and when its provenance is the Eurosceptic camp, often with ulterior motive. But the 'superior European model' line increasingly has the aura of ostrich-like, head in-the-sand blinkeredness.

A series of Commission reports has admitted that the EU is falling way behind on the types of research and development essential to longer-term growth potential. Levels of educational attainment remain a serious concern. South Korea now spends nearly 50 per cent more per pupil on education than do EU member states. Ernst and Young's reports on market attractiveness show that the EU has become markedly less enticing to investors.[2] Many European services are migrating to India. The EU is already behind China in the development of renewable energy technology.

By 2020, Asia will be a larger exporter than the EU for the first time in several centuries. In 2008, Asia surpassed the EU in research and development spending. Under 10 per cent of the EU budget goes on achieving the stated aim of enhancing Europe's global competitiveness. Look at a country like Spain, whose pre-crisis decade of growth was

2 Ernst and Young, *Reinventing European growth. European attractiveness survey,* London, 2009.

fuelled by public works and construction, not factors more directly conducive to long-term competitiveness.

The EU social model has not provided either job security or equality as a trade-off for market dynamism. Rather, its lack of market dynamism has contributed to rising inequality and declining job security. Rising economies and the USA have generated more new jobs and integrated immigrants more fully into their labour markets than have EU member states. Much less support is provided in Europe to assist worker mobility and retraining. Of course, much variation exists between member states' respective economic models; those that are open and competition-oriented, such as Denmark and Finland, are those that have the lowest levels of inequality. But despite this, governments see general flexibility and openness as endangering rather than promoting social justice.[3]

The social impact of the 'European model' is not quite as harmonious as popular legend assumes. The prevalence of unprotected contracts offered to younger workers combines with the impending pensions squeeze to stoke an inter-generational conflict that will be a central issue in future European political debate. In debates over how to respond to this and reposition Europe in the global economy, member states are splintering into different groups, with deepening divisions between three varieties of capitalism: market, coordinated and Mediterranean.[4] Retirement rules have still not

---

3 Anthony Giddens, *Europe in the Global Age*, Polity Press, Cambridge, 2007, p. 27.

4 Peter Hall and David Soskice (eds), *Varieties of Capitalism: The Institutional Foundations of Comparative Advantage*, Oxford University Press, Oxford, 2001.

been made more flexible, so that retirement becomes more of a right and less of an obligation imposed by the state at a single, common age.

Moreover, can we really be confident that the regulatory market model is still of sufficient allure to represent the basis of European soft power? While other regions have taken up many EU technical regulations, this is not necessarily a source of economic power. European states have lost market share in many countries even as these have adopted more EU regulations. It is a mistake to conflate the role played by the EU as an inspiration, on the one hand, and the nature of its power, on the other.

Moreover, in countries such as Turkey the alignment with EU technical standards and trade rules has reached a plateau. This suggests a slow decline in influence even at the level of mutual recognition of technical regulations of the single market. The EU discourse is beginning to sound like a stuck record in insisting that 'enlargement is the most successful foreign policy ever' and that it is appropriate to follow the same model of exporting regulatory rules beyond candidate countries too. The Commission proudly boasts, for instance, that over one hundred subcommittees operate under the standard agreements it oversees in the EU's neighbourhood policy, reflecting what it insists is 'the worldwide acceptance of the EU regulatory model'.[5]

The fact that many states take on board some EU labelling

---

5   Commission of the European Communities, 'Taking stock of
    the European neighbourhood policy', Communication from
    the Commission to the European Parliament and the Council,
    COM(2010) 207, European Commission, Brussels, 12 May 2010, p. 7.

standards might be a source of pride, but it is largely irrelevant to shoring up European power in the world. The EU has confused these two things. The spread of EU technical rules and standards may smooth investment but global companies adapt anyway to a range of international regulations. The constant referring to the EU as a 'regulatory superpower' is a muddle-headed syllogism.

There are many aspects of the Greek – and subsequently more general – debt crisis that lie well beyond the scope of this book; but its international repercussions are central. Think of the underlying causes of this crisis to get an idea of just how far it may weaken the EU's international unity and credibility. At the heart of Greek profligacy has been the country's abiding nepotism; not especially helpful to EU strictures of good economic governance in the developing world. And when this crisis has been about the massive surplus–deficit imbalances *within* the eurozone, it has clearly been harder for the EU to wield influence over imbalances in the broader global economy. The cuts and turmoil associated with the 750 billion euro rescue package agreed in May 2010 are hardly likely to benefit the soft power of the EU's social market economy. Talk abounds of German opinion becoming more hostile to the EU, and the spirit of unity weakening. Spillover to the EU's broader international economic role appears inevitable.

Crisis I: paradigm regression[6]

Unsurprisingly, nothing has focused attention on Europe's decline more than the financial crisis that erupted in 2008. If this crisis has hastened and deepened the drift of economic power from West to East, the way in which European governments have deliberated over their recovery plans reveals much about their judgement regarding how such decline might best be arrested. The crisis was the progeny of vertiginous market failure, and several European leaders and ministers have ceded to the temptation to pontificate melodramatically on the 'end of global capitalism'.

Mostly, however, European governments have cautioned more soberly against overreaction. At least formally, they have concurred that the gains offered by market liberalisation must not be jettisoned, but combined with more robust regulation and redistribution. And yet beneath such fine and balanced sentiment, in practice many elements of European post-crisis economic strategy risk unduly reversing market openness and integration. The justifiable and necessary search for better regulation has morphed into market-ordering interventionism that stifles the essential spirit of economic liberalism.

Phase one of Europe's economic crisis centred on the pathologies of the banking sector. The financial crisis has engendered much agreement that markets must be complemented by more constraining regulation of the financial sector. Cross-border liberalisation is an inherently unstable

---

6   The author is grateful to Philip Whyte for input on the remaining sections of this chapter.

ship in the absence of parallel cooperation on regulation. Most of the substantive reaction to the crisis has indeed been of a regulatory vein. The EU was quick to create new regulatory bodies after the crisis – a European Banking Authority, a European Insurance and Occupational Pensions Authority and a European Securities and Markets Authority. This putative European System of Financial Supervision is for now not centralised supranationally but built around cooperation between national authorities. But still, this regulatory dimension, accompanied by demand-stimulating redistribution, constituted the most substantive response to the crisis.

Many commentators and policymakers have argued that the EU can regain influence by designing a new model of financial supervision – the point being that this will be an influence based on demonstrating new forms of regulation rather than on outward-looking interdependence. But as the crisis has not forced member states to converge their national systems of financial regulation, the weight and pull of a pan-European financial system remain elusive.

In general, the new financial regulations introduced in the wake of the banking crisis do not make the distinction between high-risk transactions (which need better oversight) and low-risk ones (which should not be stifled). The House of Lords has expressed concern that the Commission's new derivatives regulation extends its scope so wide that it over-regulates 'derivatives used by non-financial businesses that have little effect on financial stability'.[7] Moreover, despite

---

7   House of Lords, European Union Committee, 'The future regulation of derivatives markets: is the EU on the right track?', 10th Report of Session 2009–10, House of Lords, London, 23 March 2010, p. 1.

G20 injunctions to cooperate, there has in practice been a shift back to national forms of differentiated regulation, as each state seeks better models of protective self-assurance.

A similar danger exists in the new Alternative Invest-ment Fund Managers directive, which has occasioned sharp debate between the UK and France, in particular. The main (as yet undecided) draft of the directive acts as covert protectionism in obliging non-European investment funds to adopt more stringent leverage ratios in order to operate in EU markets. Its scope is so wide as to impose restric-tions on the whole range of well-established investment funds, whose actions had nothing to do with the genesis of the crisis, as opposed to solely 'alternative' hedge funds. Concerns have been raised that it will also have the effect of restraining European investment in emerging markets, by placing restrictions on the amount of investment Europeans can place in funds outside the Union.[8]

In a move that shocked its EU partners, Germany followed up discussions on the directive in May 2010 with a unilat-eral ban on short selling. During the summer of 2010 the leading French and German business associations criticised their respective governments for strangling the credit vital to recovery through over-regulation.[9] European govern-ments failed to win agreement for a banking levy at the G20 summit in June 2010.

The broad aims of the new system of financial regula-tion and the varied packages of fiscal stimulus were entirely

---

8   *Financial Times*, 14 May 2010.
9   *Financial Times*, 15 June 2010, p. 6.

proper. Governments' innovative thinking and timely reaction in 2008 and 2009 saved the European economy from what could easily have been a far more severe beating. Of course, much debate revolved around governments' insistence on shepherding their economies through the recession with national stimulus packages rather than a unified, pan-European recovery plan. But however desirable a European sharing of resources pumped into the economic system may have been, the main shortcoming is in fact a different one: the understandable priority attached to short-term recovery has crowded out measures whose importance in tempering Europe's relative decline is likely to be far greater over the longer term.

Better and more coordinated regulation is undoubtedly needed. But to suggest that the pre-crisis situation was one of unfettered financial markets is an exaggeration. Even in the UK, by 2009 the state accounted for 48 per cent of national income. Many key parts of Europe's financial services sector remained closed to cross-border integration, while over fifty regulatory bodies policed financial markets.

The failure in the 2000s to open up the European services sector contributed to the fragility of separate national EU economies in confronting the financial crisis.[10] Yet European governments and the Brussels institutions have reached the opposite conclusion, namely that market integration has in a generic sense proceeded *too* far. One influential financial adviser observes that the US response to the crisis has

---

10 Hugo Brady, 'The EU must learn from its mistakes over the past decade', *CER Insight*, Centre for European Reform, London, 23 December 2009.

been designed to save the market system, many aspects of the European response to 'turn off' the market.[11] While it has become fashionable to talk of a paradigm shift to a new economic strategy, all this looks suspiciously like a regression to models already tried – and failed. If the crisis has belittled European standing in many emerging and developing nations it is in large part because, when faced with their own crisis, EU member states royally ignored the very strictures against state interventionism to which they had subjected other countries for many years.

The size of the European GDP cake accounted for by the state has jumped since the outbreak of the crisis. The new team of European commissioners installed in 2009 tilts economic portfolios away from liberals. Commission President José Manuel Barroso and others in his team have come to advocate laxity in state aid rules. Even if the single market has not been dismantled, parts of it are certainly in abeyance. Former commissioner Mario Monti's proposal that market liberalisation be completed in return for fiscal cooperation has not been taken up with enthusiasm; some member states are not keen on the former part of the quid pro quo, others are not keen on the latter.

Curiously, while the banking crisis weakened Europe, it also reinvigorated a continental conviction in 'the European model' in contradistinction to 'Anglo-Saxon capitalism'. For all the talk of a 'state capitalism' taking shape in the 'second

11 Avinash Persaud, 'The locus of financial regulation', in Andrew Cooper and Paola Subacchi (eds), 'Global economic governance in transition', *International Affairs*, 86(3), special edition, May 2010, p. 639.

world' as a challenge to Western liberalism, government now assumes a larger share of the economy in Europe than in any other region.[12] The positive dimensions of that social model (or, more accurately, variety of social models) must indeed be preserved and strengthened. But as the crisis moved into its second stage a heavier dose of humility was required.

Crisis II: sovereign debt

In remarkably little time broad agreement over the need for fiscal stimulus has given way to concern over unsustainable levels of public debt. Up to early 2010, fiscal responsibility was under increasing strain. Many advocated the creation of eurobonds to help finance a larger EU budget. Proposals for fiscal centralisation were back on the agenda. The focus was on how much should be spent, rather than on resurrecting abandoned market reforms. The Stability and Growth Pact was by then interpreted so loosely that its strictures on deficit and debt limits held little credibility as a disciplining tool. The euro clearly encouraged deficits by bringing down interest rates in southern European countries.

This all changed when the Greek debt crisis erupted in 2010. In response to a crisis generated by the lack of private sector prudence, governments' own prudence was now being questioned. The German government insisted that financial support would be extended to Greece only under extremely restrictive conditions. It also insisted on IMF assistance, which for many member states undermined a basic tenet

---

12 Alberto Alesina and Francesco Giavazzi, *The Future of Europe: Reform or Decline*, MIT Press, Cambridge, MA, 2008, p. 17.

of European solidarity. Germany claimed it would refuse point blank to contemplate a form of economic governance that would oblige it to stimulate demand in the name of assisting southern European economies. Reflecting ongoing differences with France, however, under the rescue package eventually agreed the European Central Bank (ECB) was pressed to pump huge amounts of money into the European economy.

What concerns us here is the impact of this second phase on the EU's international standing. Two prejudicial effects flow from the way in which European governments have approached the sovereign debt challenge.

First, the crisis has undermined European influence over the global macroeconomic fall-out from the crisis. As the dust settles from the financial crisis, Europe is clearly in a more defensive frame of mind as trends point towards the USA–China axis now being the key shaper of the global economy. EU influence over the question of China revaluing its currency has been zero. Debates over the future global reserve currency will not be determined by the West.

No common European position has taken shape over the fundamental need for better equilibrium between surplus and deficit countries, Germany aligning more with the reticence of Asian export-surplus countries to accept new obligations in this direction. Indeed, China is doing little more than following key tenets of Germany's export-led model – in the face of complaints from other EU member states. Many economists have argued for a further extension of IMF special drawing rights to keep liquidity high, which would lessen the need for emerging powers to run surpluses to cover Western deficits; no common EU line has emerged on such questions. Germany will not discuss a proactive EU line towards global imbalances, even though these represent far more of a serious underlying problem than the actions of hedge funds or the level of bankers' pay.[13] Other member states complain of Germany's failure to see that its reluctance to discuss global imbalances is self-defeating: as the USA can no longer run such a large deficit to offset the surplus states, without a rebalancing overall global demand must decrease.

China reportedly delayed consideration of breaking the peg of the renminbi to the dollar because of the negative effects of the euro crisis – far from helping in global rebalancing, the EU has complicated this aim. In the eyes of the outside world the EU is increasingly guilty of 'monetary nationalism'. In light of Greece's woes, the euro is increasingly not an instrument of international strength but a drain on resources. Germany is controlling the internal economic agenda but is still reluctant to accompany this with leadership over a united external policy. The emerging risk is that the paucity of solidarity on display in the euro crisis is percolating into diminished cohesion in external economic and foreign policy.

The euro is nowhere near rivalling the dollar as an international reserve currency. But in the mid-2000s it had begun to be a currency of choice for many transactions around the world. France is the member state that has pushed most strongly for fundamental reform of the international

---

13 Philip Whyte, *How to Restore Financial Stability*, Centre for European Reform, London, 2010.

monetary system, arguing for a move away from dollar primacy to a more multi-currency reserve system. As the financial crisis broke, the number of euros in circulation outside the eurozone was just over one third the number of dollars outside the USA; in 2009 the euro accounted for a quarter of total foreign exchange holdings, compared to the two-thirds held in dollars. With the new series of regulations now introduced, President Sarkozy's war on 'financial capitalism' and the Greek bailout crisis, the prospects of European power being assisted by a wider international role for the euro have been largely killed off. The ECB was reluctant to promote the euro's role as a reserve currency even before the crisis; after the turmoil of 2010 it is a question that has disappeared from the agenda.

The degree of required fiscal retrenchment is hotly debated. The June 2010 EU summit agreed that member states will face sanctions against excessive deficits – although only where the latter's 'trend' is still negative. But nothing agreed so far makes it likely that these new sanctions can succeed where the sanctions of the original Stability Pact failed. Moreover, many economists are critical of what they see as an unhealthy fixation with deficit reduction. They see Europe whipping itself into a self-defeating frenzy of collective deflation. They argue that the scale of fiscal stimulus in 2009 was not so overwhelming as to merit such harshness in 2010. This was the major difference between European governments and the USA that dominated the G20 summit in Canada in June 2010. Europe risks swinging from one extreme to the other, from panicked fiscal stimulus to overzealous fiscal contraction.

Second, the focus on fiscal discipline risks diverting attention from the underlying need to boost international competitiveness. Whatever one's view of the wisdom of fiscal correction, a vital consideration is that Europe's well-chronicled supply-side bottlenecks still get insufficient attention. Even after new austerity plans were forced upon southern European governments in mid-2010 these were accompanied by very few long-term structural reform commitments. In southern states such as Spain the underlying problem is not debt but lack of international competitiveness. Yet the euro crisis has now opened debate over whether formal treaty change is required to install new rules against fiscal indiscipline – risking another round of debate over institutional matters.

The IMF observed in May 2010 that the really profound structural reforms needed to sustain Europe's recovery had yet to begin.[14] Reforms to social systems and labour markets remain modest. Unions still wield their influence in seeking to protect those in work against struggling 'outsiders'. During the 2010 Spanish presidency, Prime Minister José Luis Rodríguez Zapatero pushed to move to the European level his (spectacularly unsuccessful) national focus on a social pact, ceding pride of place in economic decision-making to the unions. One of the crisis's most colourful anecdotes came when Spain set its intelligence services on the heels of 'Anglo-Saxon speculators' with some supposed grudge against the Iberian country – anything rather than just getting to work in implementing overdue reforms.

---

14 International Monetary Fund, *Regional Economic Outlook: Europe*, IMF, Washington, DC, May 2010.

In March 2010 the EU agreed a new strategy, dubbed EU2020, designed to reverse the decline in Europe's international competitiveness. This replaces the Lisbon strategy which over the preceding decade quite unequivocally failed in its stated aim of boosting European dynamism. But the new strategy adds little that is qualitatively upgraded. It establishes a set of new targets to be met by 2020. And a process of slightly firmer peer pressure is set up to nudge member states towards these goals. But a new set of targets hardly suffices if broader economic policies continue drifting in the wrong direction. The disconnect between EU2020 and the evolving structure of foreign policy coordination is striking. The new External Action Service is not harnessed in any tangible way to dovetail with a broader strategy aimed at stemming Europe's international decline.

The danger is that by focusing on the 2020 horizon the EU just delays the implementation of necessary reforms. Access to EU funds has not been made strictly conditional on pro-competitiveness reforms being undertaken. EU2020 once again implies that solutions flow top-down from government targets, rather than from individual dynamism. In the words of one expert: the logic is prescriptive rather than proscriptive – that is, EU2020 is based on the arbitrary imposition of identical targets for very different states instead of renewing the single market spirit of prohibiting obstacles to healthy competition between member states.[15]

The EU budget is still backward looking. The EU's much-

---

15 Fredrik Erixon, *The Case against Europe's 2020 Agenda*, policy brief 01/2010, European Centre for International Political Economy.

trumpeted Global Adjustment Fund offers mainly remedial social protection. Ten times more is allocated from the EU budget to agriculture than to research and development; twice as much is granted to boost social safety nets than goes on R&D. At the end of July 2010, Spain, Germany and Poland rejected a Commission proposal to reduce state aid to the coal industry. Only Finland and Sweden have met the Lisbon strategy's R&D target. The design of the next budget from 2014 will be crucially important.

A strong assumption has emerged that overarching European strategy will be driven by the shift to a low-carbon economy. This is widely conceived as a kind of prospective second Industrial Revolution, and one in which the EU is seen as holding pole position. The view that sustainable energy represents an area of future comparative advantage is certainly an extremely optimistic one. The presumption among European policymakers is that the move to low carbon further tilts the balance against market models. All the talk is of new 'green industrial strategies', with lists of new forms of state intervention, but little on the importance of market signals. The EU has until now accounted for nearly a third of all 'green patents', but has now begun to lose ground. Senior officials admit that the incipient EU approach to the economics of renewables is based much more on regulations than on open market incentives. State support will indeed be crucial in this sector. But in its desperation to establish a key presence in the development of renewable energy sources, the EU shows signs of resurrecting 'infant industry'-type protection. While European producers need open global markets to export renewables technology, governments have attached little importance to such trade stimulation. Ideas have been raised for a 'green free trade area', but have not been supported by several EU member states.

Globalism defeated

In the aftermath of the financial crisis the EU has become more protectionist. Even in the run-up to the crisis, Nicolas Sarkozy was baldly stating that 'Globalisation requires us to reinvent everything, and give more priority to ourselves rather than to others.' In the Netherlands the rise of the right-wing Geert Wilders is as much about anti-globalism as anti-Islamism.

The new protectionism does not primarily take the form of a naked and overt restriction of trade and investment. It is more subterfuge. It is true that the monitoring group Global Trade Alert has identified 300 new protectionist measures introduced by G20 member states between the outbreak of the crisis and 2010. But the main concern is over 'behind the border' protectionism: subsidies, bailouts, 'buy national' injunctions and restrictive conditions on inward investment. Several rescue packages contained new export subsidies.[16] An emerging source of potential new protectionism is green tariffs, being pushed by the French in particular. The French government has dropped its plan for a carbon tax at the national level in order to press for a similar measure aimed against imports at the EU level. Business groups are critical that the EU has introduced no concrete measures to ensure

---

16 Kati Suominen, 'A new age of protectionism? The economic crisis and transatlantic trade policy', Brussels Forum Paper Series, German Marshall Fund, 2009, p. 23.

that protectionism cannot enter through the back door in this myriad of forms.

Even where not reverting to protectionism, the EU has significantly scaled back its efforts to stimulate trade and investment at the global level. Such efforts were already tepid prior to the crisis, as the Doha round of multilateral trade talks stood moribund. Recommendations to improve Organisation for Economic Cooperation and Development rules designed to free up investment flows have not been implemented. Differences between member states on new rules for financial supervision hinder the EU's ability to project a common position globally in favour of liberalising financial services. This is now hardly on the agenda.

Several of the EU's special protocols covering particular agricultural products have been targeted as unlawful by the WTO. Recent EU defeats in the WTO on a range of disputes from bananas to beef hormones have compounded the cooling of attitudes towards multilateral trade liberalisation. The latest EU offer on the table in the Doha round talks would still restrict developing and emerging economies in the use of safeguard mechanisms to prevent traditional and sensitive industries from complete collapse. China has made far deeper liberalisation commitments on services than has the EU; emerging economies have resorted to less behind-the-border protectionism than have European states since the beginning of the crisis.[17] Pew opinion polls show that support for international trade liberalisation is lower

---

17 Patrick Messerlin, 'How the rich OECD nations should handle the emerging giants', *Europe's World*, Spring 2010, p. 15. For general debates on international trade and the crisis, see the excellent blog of

in many European countries than on other continents – far from free trade being foisted on to other regions, the latter are being denied their desire for open markets by a fearful Europe.[18]

The EU points to its 'Aid for Trade' initiative, which is designed to strengthen poor countries' export capacity, and its Everything-but-Arms scheme, which is said to be worth 8 billion euros a year to least developed states. But it is not clear that money promised under the Aid for Trade scheme is additional to, rather than a repackaging of, existing funds. EU rules of origin remain highly restrictive in the developing world and their reform has been delayed. These rules do not reflect the globalisation of production as they require developing countries to undertake very high levels of reprocessing that they are not set up to perform. Development officials at the European Commission despair: it has proved 'a waste of time' trying to get development concerns into trade mandates. New finance provided through the IMF is a fraction of the amount of credit that has dried up as Western banks retreat from lending in emerging and developing economies.

After the G20 promised in 2009 to move to concluding the Doha round, the EU has done nothing towards this end. It has come to pin all blame for the stagnation of trade liberalisation on the Obama administration. Trade commissioner Karel de Gucht has stated clearly that the EU will not

the Global Economic Governance Group at the University of Oxford, available at http://www.globaleconomicgovernance.org/blog/.

18 Pew Global Attitudes Report 2007, http://pewglobal.org/files/pdf/258.pdf.

make any new offer to reopen the Doha talks and that the ball is in the USA's court. He has acknowledged that there is a 'complete contradiction' between the G20 commitment to conclude the Doha round and the positions that European governments adopt in private. The very same day that the September 2009 Pittsburgh G20 summit was issuing further commitments to open trade, the EU was slamming duties on a range of steel exports from the Middle East. It is amazing that so few picked up on the irony. In 2010 China has opened a whole range of anti-dumping cases against the EU within the WTO.

Indeed, the EU has quite clearly focused its efforts on a plethora of bilateral trade deals. One member-state ambassador involved in trade negotiations notes that the EU is seeking to unblock many long-stagnant bilateral trade negotiations specifically because the Doha round is now seen as a lower priority. To some degree the EU even seems to have given up on its region-to-region approach, turning instead to bilateral talks with individual countries. Most bilateral agreements are struggling to gain traction. The deal with South Korea is the nearest to being implemented, but is now subject to fierce opposition from European producers, whose lobbying has succeeded in holding up the agreement in the European Parliament. Ten member states have come out explicitly against an EU–Mercosur trade deal.

Even if not an out-and-out return to protectionism, the maxim is increasingly one of bargaining away market access in hard-headed fashion through bilateral deals, as opposed to principled support for universal liberal norms. The EU has often been cold-shouldered in its hunt for partners to sign a new generation of preferential deals. The European Roundtable of Industrialists slams this 'spaghetti bowl' of preferential bilateral trade talks as undermining the EU's competitiveness.[19] European multinationals complain that the plethora of bilateral deals does not suit their highly international structure, to the extent that it renders rules of origin more restrictive and complicated: with European firms operating across the globe such an approach of separating out supposedly key markets is very much suboptimal.

The Lisbon treaty gives the Commission some new trade-related powers, for example in the field of international investment. But it also enhances the monitoring role of the European Parliament, at a time when more MEPs are free trade sceptics. Many industrial lobbies have already targeted MEPs, aware of the latters' new powers to hold up trade liberalisation. The Commission complains that the political clauses included in EU agreements with other parts of the world are now being used as a convenient tool to delay free trade by MEPs who have never been champions of the subjects covered by these clauses, such as human rights or non-proliferation. Moreover, the Lisbon treaty leaves trade policy outside the scope of the EAS, more susceptible to the lobbying of vested interests than to a push for liberalisation as part of overarching EU geostrategy.[20]

---

19 Euractiv, 'Big business demands accountability of EU2020', Euractiv, 5 February 2010.

20 Stephen Woolcock, *The Treaty of Lisbon and the European Union as an Actor in International Trade*, Working Paper 01/2010, European Centre for International Political Economy.

Russia's decision to back away from preparing for WTO accession now hampers talks with Moscow. Talks with China have produced no new commitments – unlike China's similar talks with the USA which are very much more linked to currency diplomacy. India shows little interest while the EU cannot get its act together on services – and while the dilution of the services directive within the EU spills over to impede the EU's external offer in respect of service sector liberalisation. Several studies have concluded that for developing states the gains from south–south trade deals exceed what is now on offer from the West at the multilateral level. Many member states justify their new protectionism by pointing to the imperative for the global order of 'rebalancing' between surplus and deficit states – a shift that requires European states to cut trade deficits. In particular, Europe defends its economic protectionism by asserting that China and India are engaged in the kind of savage capitalism that Europe has left behind. The EU still refuses to grant China market economy status, which would oblige Europe to rein back its use of anti-dumping duties. In areas such as satellite navigation, incipient cooperation has given way to zero-sum competition as both the EU and China veer more towards economic mercantilism.

The trade deficit with China is a serious concern but can be exaggerated into a pretext. The magnitude of cross-border commercial flows within the EU remains far, far greater than between the Union and China. Many member states have just as large deficits with each other as with China. For example, the UK's trade deficit with China is no larger than its deficit with Germany (£5.7 compared to £5.6

billion in the year to April 2010).[21] Moreover, China's exports are largely displacing those from other Asian states, which have declined.[22] The EU's neglect of political governance also matters. For example, Chinese citizens save so much (and thus in turn demand fewer European goods) because there is no open and transparent state that provides a predictable social safety net in China – with no social safety net the economic crisis is forcing huge numbers of Chinese workers out of the big cities, raising the prospect of future social tensions.

The only way to recover influence from the crisis is for the EU to increase exports to Asian and other emerging economies, requiring much more market opening from China and others, and much more consumption on the part of Asian consumers. Yet the concessions requisite to making such progress appear absent from European international economic strategy. As Brazil rises, EU trade with the strongly performing Latin American giant has actually stagnated. The EU2020 strategy refers to the importance of broader commercial policy, but without any new initiative to suggest that this is anything other than more hollow rhetoric. Council President Herman van Rompuy has repeatedly advocated a hunkering down to defend the European social model.

The EU's export of its own regulations is increasingly

---

21 HM Revenue and Customs, *Overseas Trade Statistics*, April 2010, available at www.uktradeinfo.com.

22 Frederik Erixson and Rajiv Sally, 'Defensiveness and fragmentation in trade policy', in Loukas Tsoukalis, *The EU in a World in Transition: Fit for What Purpose?*, Policy Network, London, 2009, p. 103.

about shoring up a self-contained economic identity and using political power to this end in a way that is not necessarily conducive to overall economic vibrancy. By adopting such regulations, in areas like environmental standards, non-EU partners increasingly complain that they incur all the costs of these rules without the quid pro quo gain of untrammelled access to European markets. One expert calculates that 80 per cent of such regulations have the effect of loading non-EU states with bureaucracy that undermines their competitiveness.[23] One Middle Eastern diplomat complains: 'we want real substance, trade and investment; the EU wants endless "frameworks"'. Southern Mediterranean states talk of the EU's 'legal colonialism' in insisting on adoption of its own market regulations. A constant complaint from non-EU states is that they have to divert too much capacity into EU regulatory committees, deflecting attention from local reform priorities.

The energy sector is perhaps the clearest case of a retraction from liberalism. The Commission has initiated a whole stream of court cases against member states pulling back from internal market rules in the energy sector. And this has a clear international effect, as supplies are negotiated on a case-by-case basis through bilateral contracts. To facilitate these, there is a clear swing back towards governments supporting their own national energy champions in a bid to gain the most favourable terms possible in international deals. In the Gulf and North Africa, member-state

---

23 Patrick Messerlin, 'Valuing our neighbours: pro-growth initiatives and the danger of exporting the wrong regulatory frameworks', in Tsoukalis, op. cit., p. 79.

governments have sought energy cooperation on the back of traditional geopolitical forms of engagement, such as security cooperation and arms sales. There is a case for the Commission to back long-term contracts to give guarantees for needed investment in energy infrastructure and storage facilities. But this is different from the engineering of European champions in a way that increasingly closes the European market to outsiders. With European oil giants now having access to a lower share of reserves than ever before, reciprocal internationalisation as opposed to Euro-autarchy has to be the only sustainable way forward in the energy sector.

All countries want to export their way out of the crisis. If none is willing to increase imports relative to exports, it is a logical impossibility for all countries to achieve this objective. Observers fear that it is this series of mutually incompatible economic strategies among developed and developing nations which portends geopolitical tension and a retreat into tit-for-tat protectionism. Looking at the nature of its international economic policies, one cannot help thinking that the EU is seeking to stem the rise of other powers – exactly the opposite of all its forward-looking, positive-sum, 'by helping rising powers we help ourselves' rhetoric.

Conclusion

The result of the financial crisis is not merely recession. It is not even simply the 'great recession' that many commentators talk of. Rather, it leaves a profoundly geopolitical afterburn. The crisis is a painfully shrill wake-up call that should leave the danger of decline pulsating in the European brain.

Economic challenges cannot be reduced to the crisis alone; but the latter does in a sense subsume or magnify the gamut of challenges with which the EU was already beginning to grapple before financial meltdown struck in 2008 and the sovereign debt crisis tested internal solidarity to its limits in 2010. The nature of Europe's response to the crisis will do much to set the course of its broader international presence for many years to come.

One line increasingly heard among Euro-diplomats is: in light of the crisis, let us focus on simply preserving what we have and making sure the whole internal edifice of unity and cooperation does not crumble. The authoritative Bruegel Institute observes that the alliance of convenience between free marketers and pro-Europeans that drove European integration from the mid-1980s has now fractured; the result of the crisis is that rising Euroscepticism and a fading faith in markets are now politically joined at the hip.[24]

Few of the liberalisation measures pursued prior to the crisis sought fundamentally to question the corrective and redistributive role of the state. The financial sector does indeed require better regulation. But concern must be raised over how far European governments are now rolling back from the core tenets of economic internationalism.

Such a drift neither correctly identifies the crisis's causes nor sets Europe up well for long-term recovery. Protectionism will not help global rebalancing; moreover, some surplus countries are among the most protectionist. All

---

24 André Sapir (ed.), 'Europe's economic priorities 2010–2015. Memos to the new Commission', Bruegel Institute, Brussels, September 2009, p. 13.

European economies were mixed economies prior to the crisis and will remain so in its wake. As Joseph Stiglitz has put it: a lot of money has been spent on simply trying to preserve the status quo rather than preparing Western economies for what will be a fundamentally different international economic and financial model.[25]

Two finely balanced policy aims must be combined in Europe's recovery plans. First, stronger European unity becomes even more imperative. But, second, such unity should not be seen as synonymous with defending 'the' European model in monolithic rigidity. This is the real danger which now rears its head. The EU talks interdependence but then seems to glorify its economic model in illusory hermetic splendour.

The EU's whole economic logic appears predicated on erecting barriers to prevent emerging states from gaining market share, instead of seeing the advent of new economic powers as something positive-sum. The EU must realise that opening up to new powers can offer absolute gains, much more real than an inevitably doomed defence of relative market shares.

Somehow, unity must be combined with flexibility. The EU is thinking in terms of size rather than adaptability; China is its model not Singapore. Setting targets as a way forward still tilts towards the notion that top-down state action is the secret to resolving Europe's economic woes. Rather, what is needed is greater agility and bottom-up

---

25 Joseph Stiglitz, 'The global economic crisis: issues for the G20 agenda', Ideas, Madrid, October 2009, p. 7.

dynamism. Far from battling 'big capital', European progressives have colluded in state support and protection for big, privileged firms against smaller entrepreneurs. The left has reacted to the crisis by reverting to an anti-liberal big-state stance, the right by questioning internationalism. Both are likely to hasten, not slow, decline.

The EU still tends to think primarily in terms of how far the European economic orbit extends, as defined by the extension of regulations. This is the wrong way to think about retaining influence. It is verging on Euro-heresy to question the 'sellability' of the EU model to other parts of the world – an abiding pillar of European group-think. But European policymakers must begin to approach the problem of economic decline from other perspectives, before Europe has nothing very attractive left to export at all.

7

Conclusions: The road less travelled

'Never let the future disturb you. You will meet it, if you must,
with the same weapon of reason which today arms you against
the present.'

Marcus Aurelius, *Meditations*

The European Union has spent a decade in almost child-like distraction. Policy challenges have arisen that, while all acutely important in their own right, have fractured and diverted the response to Europe's long-run relative decline. The amount of time and mind-numbing detail poured into debates over a new constitution were trying for even the most dedicated Euro-geek. And after so many years of these debates, the year since the passing of the Lisbon treaty has been one the EU's least fine hours: the EU's institutional structure and rules still seem to hinder more than they assist.

And, of course, with the Greek bailout and ongoing euro crisis the trend towards decline has accelerated. Saving the euro and core internal EU solidarity has for the moment quashed the prospects of more proactive, long-term thinking on Europe's international influence. Given the atonal discord of so much post-Lisbon tension and debate, perhaps the treaty should have formally changed the EU hymn from Beethoven to Schönberg.

Much comment in 2010 has been directed in a very personal and rather brutal way at Catherine Ashton. After nearly a year of exhausting infighting, the new External Action Service does not (yet) constitute a qualitative jump forward – rather it doles out positions between member states within what looks like a very traditional diplomatic set-up. Look at the presidencies of 2010 to see how little has changed. Spain prioritised a summit with Latin America, while a summit with Africa was given to the Belgian presidency to organise. Such neocolonial hangovers still muddy the waters of the EU's institutional coherence. The focus on organisational task division has if anything become even more overwhelming in 2010. One Commission director despairs that even after the Lisbon reforms the foreign policy budget is no greater than the amount spent on internal administration. Much mirth abounds among the press that the best-known fact about Herman van Rompuy is his love of Japanese haiku poetry; it is perhaps apocryphal that this is a form of verse defined by its rigid form, combined with invariably banal substance.

The invasion of Iraq was a tragic episode that rightly stirred the concerns of many Europeans. But for much of the mid-2000s it was the red rag to European anger (on both sides of the debate), which clouded our collective view of more structural changes afoot in international politics. The financial crisis has focused minds quite properly on tightening state regulation of dysfunctional markets; but one fears that this necessary fire-fighting is again diverting minds and resources from redressing longer-term, under-lying trends. In the second decade of the century, the EU must move beyond such fissiparous policymaking. It must overcome its attention deficit disorder. It is time to return to the broader sweep of history.

Diagnosis

To manage its relative decline as well as possible, Europe must first correctly diagnose its current plight. And this is no small matter, as the 'European condition' is still commonly misinterpreted. It is invariably assumed that in the ineluc-table recasting of the international order the EU has affirmed itself as the world's last cosmopolitan. And indeed, it is widely argued, too much so for its own good. Tony Judt captured the spirit of this most common of perceptions in suggesting that the EU tends to be 'very nice and very ineffective'.[1] Walter Laqueur attributes Europeans' current woes to the fact that 'they now find themselves in a world in which power politics still matter, and they are ... less prepared to engage in such politics than ever'.[2]

But this widely held sentiment is not quite right. At least some of the problems that beset European foreign policy reflect exactly the opposite trend. Europe can be faulted in most instances not for being too 'nice' but too narrowly self-centred. The very frequency with which European politi-cians insist on the EU's moral superiority and sophisticated

---

1   Tony Judt and Kristina Bozic, 'The way things are and how they might be', *London Review of Books*, 25 March 2010, p. 12.

2   Walter Laqueur, 'A crisis of wishing', *The American Interest*, July/August 2010.

approach to international affairs should make one suspect. As the aphorism runs: the more insistent the deceiver, the greater his mendacity. However firmly the assumption has embedded itself in the European psyche that we are just too ethical and liberal for our good, this does not change the fact that reality tells a contrasting story. In Chesterton's much-quoted words: fallacies don't cease to be fallacies just because they become fashions.

European Union foreign policy uneasily mixes conservative and forward-looking logics, the defensive and expansive, the inward- and outward-looking, the isolationist and the internationally engaged. Policy has the uncanny ability to contradict precisely its own ostensibly core principles. In this dual personality, much European foreign policy verges on double-think. The EU seems intent on trying to develop a foreign policy that functions while simultaneously holding mutually incompatible ideas, veering between the predatory and the passive, bypassing principled proactivism.

This book has charted developments across a number of policy areas to demonstrate two defining features in the evolution of European foreign policy. On the one hand, we increasingly see in EU policies the classic symptoms of zero-sum realism. For many diplomats this is the recipe required for navigating the post-Western world. And indeed, we have chronicled this policy trend in the EU's approach to multilateral alliance-building, international economic policy and security challenges. In the field of human rights and democracy the EU has shown itself to be more of a plati-tudinous than a principled power.

On the other hand, and sometimes sitting uneasily with

this overarching geostrategy, the conviction reigns that the best weapons in the EU's arsenal are its own *sui generis* rules and regulations. In the fields of energy, economic governance and regional cooperation the EU relies too heavily on an assumption that its international influence can be safeguarded by extending outwards its own model of integration. The coexistence of these two dynamics is the central point stressed in the first chapter: the balance between over- and under-reaction to decline differs across policy areas.

At the same time, in the complex evolution of identity politics we see a curious simultaneity of national nationalism and Euro-nationalism. Far from being exempt from chauvinism, Europe displays just such inwardness at a multiplicity of levels, with the internal and external elements of identity politics feeding off each other.

The tendency in each policy area we have looked at is to react to the risks more than to the opportunities of the emerging world order. The EU is becoming more adept at trying to shield against uncertainty than it is at seizing opportunity – the opportunity of growing market demand around the world; of other powers' capabilities rising to tackle shared security challenges; of vibrant mobilisations of citizens around the world demanding greater say over both national and international decision-making; of the fashioning of more shared and cosmopolitan identities.

Stepping back from the specific trends in each policy area, we can detect features of a common pathology that extends across the different strands of EU international strategy: the vain search for exclusivity and a doomed spirit of defensive preservation. In the economic, social, political and strategic spheres, European policies contain too much that is retrograde. Whatever other minor ailments the EU may also suffer from – which form the subject matter of many studies of European foreign policy – this is the principal diagnosis with which we must contend.

Robert Kagan's influential thesis – that Europe's weakness lies in its overdose of airy idealism and inability to pursue self-interest with assertion – has been proved wrong. The concern must be not with Europe heading naively into a world of Kantian idealism, but rather with it pulling too far *away* from such values. Kagan's critique was unduly simplistic when it first hit the headlines at the beginning of the 2000s. As he continually reasserts the same line now,[3] it seems even more blind to the direction that concrete European policies are taking.

And, related to this, it is profoundly unsatisfactory that so much focus of debate has so far been on 'why we are different from the USA'. On this question, the 'Mars versus Venus' dichotomy is unhelpful. A 'Greeks versus Romans' EU–US comparison is an exaggeration still. At most, we might talk more in terms of a European Cicero matched against an American Pompey. But whatever the most appropriate metaphor, the larger point is that the EU has been looking in the wrong direction as a very different juggernaut thunders over the horizon towards both Europe and the USA.

European power vaporises before our eyes. The EU is wrong to think that it can insulate itself from the incipient

---

3   Robert Kagan, 'The need for power', *Wall Street Journal*, 20 January 2010.

global upheaval. Pawel Swieboda writes that the 'international outlook of most European countries is shrinking, not getting bigger' – and likens this to a Freudian narcissism of small ambition.[4] To seek such insulation corrupts the most positive dimensions of the recent European experience. The metaphor comes to mind of Europe cutting off the very branch it is sitting on. *The Economist*'s Charlemagne hits the nail on the head: 'European leaders talk about things changing but in ways designed to appeal, all too often, to the side of Europe that is old, tired and anxious.'[5] Jean Monnet himself pessimistically predicted many times that his creation would end up with a constant tendency towards judging itself to be self-sufficient both economically and politically. Sadly, he is being proved right.

Remedies: five guiding principles

The EU's crisis is deep and requires a change of direction with some urgency. But there is no need for phoenix-like rebirth – an image that politicians' prophecies sometimes conjure up. Perspective is required. It sometimes seems as if the EU has passed in the blink of an eye from one extreme to the other, from being lionised as poster child of post-Westphalian international relations to being a basket case. It was never the former; it is not the latter.

On taking office, Catherine Ashton said her aim was to 'keep the traffic moving' – responding to the jibe that she

---

4   Pawel Swieboda, 'Recapture the ground', *Global Europe*, available at http://www.globeurope.com/standpoint/recapture-the-ground, posted 6 April 2010.

5   *The Economist*, 12 December 2009, p. 36.

had insufficient star power to stop the traffic in Washington or Beijing – and focus on practical progress and cooperation.[6] This attitude strikes exactly the right note. But has she lived up to this admirable pragmatism of ambition?

Unfortunately, a year after the entry into force of the Lisbon treaty and its supposedly empowering foreign policy set-up, the EU continues to be confused and in disarray over its global identity. It was inevitable that a period of time should be spent working on the detailed fixtures and fittings of the Lisbon architecture. But the results of a decade of time-consuming and resource-draining effort to 'get the institutions right' have been disappointing. It is, of course, understandable that priority has been attached to tempering the turmoil of the euro crisis. But this also cannot justify a neglect of longer-term geostrategic challenges.

Proceeding from a more fine-toothed diagnosis of what is currently wrong with European foreign policy, some necessary lines of action emerge. These require significant change, but can in most cases build on rather than disposing of the strengths latent within existing EU instruments. Here are five guiding principles for what the EU should do to change its current approach to foreign policy:

1 Get over the fixation with institutional structures

European diplomats have been traumatised by Henry Kissinger's 1970s taunt that he had no single number to call to 'speak to Europe'. This is one of the most frequently cited quotes in work on European foreign policy. But it distorts

---

6   *Time*, 8 March 2010.

the most pressing challenges. As important as whether there are one, two or three key numbers is what the people on the end of the phone have to say. After all, Europe had Mr Kissinger's single line to call, but what he had to say about world politics proved to be so disastrous it might have helped to have some alternative numbers. And when Javier Solana's line was installed, Americans and others often hung up after lengthy calls, not always clear what the EU's intentions really were. This is not to say that having a single voice is not helpful. But it is not a panacea; its importance is often played up to compensate for the absence of more forward-looking debate on repositioning Europe within the world.

The endless debates over institutional structures and bureaucratic politicking reverberate little beyond a Brussels echo-chamber. This is not to say that the reforms of the Lisbon treaty are not important or positive. But the amount of political capital member states expend on these institutional questions – getting 'their' men and women into key places, trading off bits of their preferred structural vision with those of other states – remains disproportionate. It nourishes a deeply unfavourable characterisation common around the globe: the EU as the world's patron of procrastination. In the long run, will all this really represent anything more than an extremely elaborate arrangement of deckchairs on the good ship *Euro-Titanic*?

2 Unity is a means not an end in itself
The ubiquitous instinct – at least outside the backward-looking circles of Euroscepticism – is to repeat ad nauseum the mantra of 'more Europe'. But more external coordination

is not an end in itself. It is not desirable if it sets forth towards mistaken aims. It is of course *ceteris paribus* desirable for Europe to act in unity. But a specious unity is not necessarily preferable to a degree of plurality that helps Europe debate options and find its way through the thicket of a recalibrated international system – as long as such plurality stops short of mutual weakening.

The standard line is: Europe must be united, and then it can take its place in a new world order alongside the USA and China. Fine, but unity is not in itself sufficient. The overwhelming focus on the 'single voice' is far too unidimensional a reasoning. We must stop thinking purely in terms of 'structural weight' in this sense, and pay more heed to qualitative sources of influence in global politics. And, on this score, it remains to be demonstrated that there really is a naturally innate European way of conducting international politics. A key guiding principle must be for the EU to deepen its reflection on the kind of substantive responses required to temper decline – and *then* to judge the value of coordination in pursuit of those responses. This is not meant as a message that is sceptical of deeper European integration; rather, simply that horse and cart must be properly ordered.

3 Forget trying to replicate the EU model

The EU cannot merely rely passively on the supposed magnetic appeal of its own model as a substitute for a proactive foreign policy. It has done so for too long, seduced by the success of several rounds of enlargement into thinking this can be a generalised guiding principle for its global influence. Such an approach appears both too 'heavy' to afford the EU strategic agility, and not always in tune with the priorities of non-European partners. To the south and to the east, this long-standing pillar of European foreign policy has at least sometimes become an obstacle to, rather than a source of, effective engagement.

A more flexible form of conducting international relations must be allowed to come to the fore. The EU still tends to think in terms of concentric circles spreading outwards from Europe-as-centre. It needs to begin from a template of multiple centres of power, and then think how to exert influence from this basis.

The EU's commitment – at least rhetorical – to rules-based cooperation is admirable and necessary. But such a laudable aim is often held to be synonymous with requiring others to sign up to the kind of formal rules-based agreements with which the EU feels familiar in terms of its own internal functioning. So, for instance, the EU would do well to temper its fixation with contractual agreements as the basis for all strategic partnerships – as these include many aspects that burden more than they incentivise rising powers. Strategic partnerships must be what they indicate: strategic rather than technical; and a two-way partnership rather than an effort to 'Europeanise' others as a presumptuous solution to all geopolitical ills.

4 Move from European to universal values

The notion of EU foreign policy peddling certain norms and values is widely berated today as neo-imperialist. Certainly, greater flexibility and humility are required from Europe in learning from other regions' values. And yet the tendency to let pass horrendous abuses in other parts of the world, snug under a convenient cloak of political correctness, should be a source of shame. Any number of extremely clever theories and schools of thought can be and have been devised to justify, even extol, such inaction. But at root this still boils down to standing aside spinelessly and blocking out the pained pleas of those suffering repression around the world. Discretion and respect for other political values and systems are absolutely necessary; but these principles now bleed freely into cynicism and hypocrisy. Supporting democratic breakthrough is now seen by the EU as almost akin to sedition. Often, not acting can be the most neo-imperial thing of all. The real neo-imperialism is pretending not to interfere but surreptitiously doing what is necessary to maintain insalubrious friends in power. This is something many European governments have come to excel at.

Isaiah Berlin famously argued that universalism entailed greater, not diminished, pluralism: liberal politics was merely the framework to allow different peoples the chance to realise their own preferences, their own individuality, their own 'idiosyncratic, unique, particular ends'.[7] Values must not be preached but approached from the point of view of common interests with peoples across different regions. To borrow in metaphorical terms from the hard sciences, in its approach to values the EU must move from a logic of fission to fusion – from a notion of values spreading outwards from a European nucleus to that of a universal demand for rights

---

7   Berlin, op. cit., pp.11 and 47.

coalescing through support from many different quarters. Amity and non-dogmatic encouragement of liberal values can and should be combined.

The EU has had its policy back to front. It has been increasingly tolerant of illiberal core political values, while exporting its own very *sui generis* detailed, technical institutional frameworks. It should reverse this, prioritising basic liberal political rights, while stepping back from 'selling' its own governance norms and regulations. After all, can we really take such satisfaction that a given regime agrees to stick EU eco-labelling on its food while continuing to murder its own citizens? Is there not something askew in our priorities here?

Reverting to universalism means according greater weight to the citizens beyond Europe's borders, as opposed to granting their leaders the status of such absolutely privileged interlocutors. The brilliant Ismail Kadare offers us the allegorical tale of China's Great Wall being rebuilt not by the Ming dynasty but by the tribal leaders beyond – the latter fearing the loss of their own power through the spread of the dynasty's modernity.[8]

5 Get strategic about ideals and values
The idea that Europe should prioritise normative values as part of its own search for international security is also on the back foot. It is an idea seen as inimical to European self-interest. Many would also deem it slightly ludicrous in its degree of ambition, when an enfeebled EU might – to clean

---

8   Ismail Kadare, *The Great Wall*, Canongate, Edinburgh, 2007.

up the popular phrase – struggle even to organise inebriation in a brewery.

In terms of self-interest, the EU must remember that 'spheres of influence' thinking was what landed the continent in the turmoil of its brutal twentieth century. Returning to such a way of seeing the wider world is hardly auspicious. A patient but firm adherence to core liberal values is the best guarantor of Europe's own prosperity and stability over the long term. The shape of the post-Western world does not invalidate this argument, but makes it more convincing. Timothy Garton Ash captures this in his appeal for a 'realistic idealism'.[9] The sceptic will ask whether it is not foolishly naive to advocate quiet power in an unquiet world. But is this not exactly when such virtue is required?

None of this should imply adhering inflexibly to some pristine, ideal template of liberal world order, inattentive to others' ideas and preferences. But the basic vision that links together the needed change in direction across all the policy areas we have looked at in this book is that of a return to at least the core values of liberalism. In adopting such a vision, a certain degree of bravery will be required of policymakers. As already noted, the instinct in a crisis is to think of tightened state control as the solution. The current juncture compounds the EU's tendency towards such control. In tight spots, the liberal path is the less travelled. It goes against the reflex to micro-engineer solutions. Liberalism breeds a politics that is messy and unstable, but also one that is associated with

---

9   Timothy Garton Ash, 'As threats multiply and power fragments, the coming decade cries out for realistic idealism', *Guardian*, 30 December 2009.

energy, dynamism and the overcoming of stagnant tradition. Liberalism above all invests faith in individuals' potential.

It is often thought that Europe is divided by two opposing notions of liberty: British negative liberty versus the continental advocacy of more state-directed positive liberty. This fault-line is rooted in history, and is the source of so much that has determined Europe's history since the Middle Ages. But a combination of these two visions can be Europe's compass for negotiating the constricted rapids of the new world order.

John Stuart Mill himself recognised that freedom is not purely personal autonomy; that civic spirit and participation are required; and that a vital public-state contribution is required to widen the scope of liberty. Some degree of state direction and intervention is needed to underpin negative liberty and need not dilute personal autonomy. Liberalism has become confused. In the USA it is seen as meaning dirigiste leftism. In Europe it is pilloried as right-wing free market dogma. It is neither. The mid-twentieth-century roots were not only Hayek but leftists such as Harold Laski. The key is a distinction between (desired) individuality and (unwelcome) individualism. Two unfortunate associations must be overcome: many supporters of economic and cultural statism pass as progressives but share much with some extremely illiberal ideologies of previous epochs; free market economic liberalism has in its turn also been associated with centralising state control and narrowed civic liberty in social and political spheres. Neither reflects what the great liberal thinkers like Berlin and Mill were about.[10] A

10 Wilson, op. cit.

first step must be to rescue liberalism from such confusion, as a prelude to establishing it as the guiding principle for managing Europe's decline.

Remedies: ten policies

So much for guiding principles. How should these be translated into concrete policy changes? It is clear from the preceding chapters that much policy will be a matter of patiently and undramatically living up to existing rhetorical commitments. But some creative thinking might also help catalyse. In the name of spurring debate, here are ten concrete policy ideas. Some are deliberately audacious, in an effort to convey the fact that the EU's plight does require us to throw at least a little caution to the wind and toss around some new ideas.

1. An overarching strategy should be prepared to lay out a road map for managing decline. At present, different dimensions of such a strategy are scattered between a variety of thematic efforts in a way that does not add up to a comprehensive policy. In particular, at present the economic and strategic elements of a necessary 'Dealing with Decline' strategy are quite patently not joined together. The European Security Strategy and the EU2020 initiative, for instance, simply do not relate to each other. A better vision is needed of how the political dimensions of EU foreign policy will work to back up the stated aims of international economic policy. The documents that exist at present of course talk about the scale of future challenges, but in far too generic a way

for their deliverables and commitments to be tightly moulded around specific indicators of decline. A new 'Dealing with Decline' strategy should be managed from within the External Action Service, helping to overcome the fact that at present this diplomatic hub has no locus over economic issues. The new strategy must include concrete yardsticks so that progress can be measured and governments held to account.

2. The EU should once and for all bite the bullet and offer comprehensive free trade both at the multilateral level and through its plethora of new bilateral negotiations. In return, the EU should require partners signing these bilateral agreements to work with European governments to deepen commitments to human rights, democracy and cooperative security within multilateral institutions. European negotiators must be obliged to show that they have used political capital to progress on these issues rather than on bludgeoning partners into signing readmission and counterterrorist clauses. Of course, the call for more symmetrical free trade is nothing new. But what would shake up the current stasis would be for a series of systematic quid pro quos to be offered to the vested interests that have for many, many years kept EU policy so protectionist: this is where the kinds of initiatives provided for under the 2020 strategy might come into play, funded by what must become a much more forward-looking EU budget.

3. On the question of enlargement, one's instinct is to repeat the plea simply for the EU to 'get on with it'. Given the reality of some member-state resistance to

doing this at present, some kind of trade-off is needed. The Balkan states can be absorbed relatively painlessly in the medium term. But Turkey and Ukraine may require a two-step strategy. They should be promised membership in unequivocal terms but to be realised only in the medium term. This will give nervous member states time to digest the changes of the Lisbon treaty, but send a clear message to both Ukraine and Turkey that they will join. In this way the EU can bargain the certainty of its promise for preparatory time. To take the politics out of the process, an independent assessment should be made of the two states' compliance with the entry criteria, in addition to the yearly Commission reports.

4. Instead of deploying quite a number of CSDP missions that consist of no more than a handful of personnel and have shown themselves to be utterly ineffectual, the EU should choose to send only one mission per year – but to make this sizeable enough to really make a difference. It should be deployed in a way that fits tightly with the EU's overall global strategic vision, rather than chosen on the basis of apparently random criteria as happens at present. The mission must demonstrate that it is attacking the political core of the conflict in question. The mission must have a clear political, not military, lead and must be conjoined with a well-worked-out political vision for resolving instability. The military element must serve a political lead, rather than the latter being added as an afterthought as at present.

5. Strategic Partnership Plus. The contractual strategic

partnerships the EU has rushed to agree with rising countries around the world are too numerous, too scattered and too overloaded. The EU tends to throw into these agreements everything bar the kitchen sink in the name of comprehensiveness. The result is that progress becomes hard to measure, efforts are dispersed and easy issues chosen over those where cooperation is most necessary. The EU tends to reach reflexively for 'more official-level meetings' as a solution to everything – despite the fact that its foreign policy frameworks already suffer from meeting overload. It is too late to undo the large number of partnerships already signed. But the EU should be obliged to select in each case one big issue on which cooperation will be pursued and tangible progress demonstrated – a kind of Strategic Partnership Plus. The priority issue identified in each partnership would receive greater diplomatic attention and resources, and be subject to more rigorous scrutiny from the European Parliament and national legislatures.

6. The bilateralism monitor. Principles for an outward-looking, enlightened and cosmopolitan approach to decline are readily enumerated in formal EU documents. A big problem is that member states simply ignore all such principles in their bilateral policies. They should be constrained from doing so. An independent body should be set up, containing national and European parliamentarians, experts, civil society representatives and business executives, to monitor such pernicious bilateralism. Where, at the end of each year, a member state is found by this body egregiously to have flouted

the core principles of an internationalist response to dealing with decline, their actions should be publicised through some form of yearly ranking.

7. The External Action Service should be obliged to show each year where it has in a tangible manner helped advance human rights and democracy in ten countries. It should be asked to demonstrate such progress to a committee of national and European parliamentarians. Some form of independent audit should be carried out of the official claims that progressive reforms are advanced simply through talking to authoritarian regimes and offering the latter juicy aid and trade benefits. If this cannot be demonstrated, our diplomats should be held to account.

8. The EU insists it 'listens to local voices' around the world, unlike the sinister top-down USA. So, it should be forced to prove it. Each year a Global Citizens Forum should meet in Brussels and democratically select policy initiatives it wishes the EU to adopt. The EU would promise to take on board one such preferred initiative each year to demonstrate that it is genuine about taking into consideration social concerns around the world. Should it refuse to do so, it would be patently apparent how hollow its professed 'Kantian multilateralism' really is.

9. Muslim minorities should be involved on a systematic basis with the EU foreign policy machinery. In return for better tolerance of their rights and identities within Europe, they would be given the opportunity to contribute to EU foreign policy aims in North Africa

and the Middle East. While they protest their 'moderate' nature within domestic political debates, they should be offered the chance and positive incentives for enhancing the same values beyond Europe.

10. A clear set of guidelines should be drawn up on engagement with 'difficult' regimes. These should work towards criteria for conditions that should be attached to engagement. They need not undermine the basic EU preference for positive engagement. But they must establish some objective red lines for a third country's behaviour, beyond which such engagement will be reduced. The guidelines must provide a clear schema for responses to particular kinds of human rights abuses and a mapping of different degrees of sanction appropriate to different types of situation. They must include penalties for member states that contravene the guidelines through their bilateral aid, trade and diplomatic instruments. It is of course the case that an overly rigid template should be avoided and that flexibility is quite proper in dealing with vastly differing states around the world. But at present a virtually complete lack of any objectivity in determining EU responses undermines European credibility.

Policymakers will likely think some of these ideas completely off the wall. And yet some form of new thinking and fresh ideas is certainly required to galvanise the EU into action. At least some means of shaking up a comfortable foreign policy elite need to be found. If Harold Macmillan was right to brood that foreign policy must choose between the cliché and the indiscretion, the EU excels at the former, and could do with at least a modest pinch of the latter.

Lamentably, what passes for 'new' thinking in European foreign policy circles today is, when one scratches beneath the surface of slightly modified terminology, deeply revisionist. What passes for out-of-the-box thinking is in fact a leap out of one analytical box straight into another – one sitting musty and abandoned in the corner for many years. It is a move deeply inimical to the foreign policy values that European political elites have long sold to their populations.

Prognosis

With these considerations in mind, what, then, are the prospects for the European Union's international influence? If the EU modifies its strategic approaches will it make much difference anyway? Are the trends not so overwhelmingly unfavourable that Europe is condemned come what may to be a fettered and decadent power?

It should be stressed that there is much in current international trends that is not set in stone. It is true that, *contra* Thomas Friedman,[11] Europe's world at present hardly looks emboweringly and enticingly flat; it is certainly rather many-sided, jagged and scarred. But while the challenges are daunting, there is still time to play a role in moulding the contours of the emerging world order. There is as yet no single paradigm that is clearly established as the defining new structure for international relations. We live in a moment of

---

11 Thomas Friedman, *The World Is Flat: A Brief History of the Twenty-first Century*, Farrar, Straus & Giroux, New York, 2005.

flux, in which dimensions of several dynamics coexist – new great-power rivalry, transnational links and some activity remaining around the notion of universal values, an incipient G2, non-polarity mixed with multipolarity, traces still of US hegemony, and religious-cum-civilisational differences (real or imagined). In this melee, it is the time to shape, not accept any trends as definitive.

A necessary first step towards doing this is that the EU's foreign policy establishment recognise the path they have set out on leads downhill to a dead end. That realisation is not yet apparent. As a plane's speed can be appreciated better from outside than from within the cabin, so Europe's decline has been noted with greater perspicacity beyond the continent's own borders. At least in their institutional logic, the policy options debated today represent a continual tinkering with the acting and props in the same play, when it is a new work that is required. Recalling Hegel's mythical owl of Minerva, the EU seems intent on perfecting its capacity to deal with an already departing era.

What Europe need not become obsessed with is a loss in power of a deeply traditional, militarist kind. The common tendency is to assume that it is in this domain that Europe's decline is most alarming. But this is not the case. Influence in the post-Western world will and must be derived from other sources. Europe must obviously remain strong in its defensive capabilities. But the real urgency is to nourish the deeper roots of international influence: those that depend on the kind of global values and vision that Europe stands for, and the degree of respect it commands as a result. One of Machiavelli's celebrated quips that recent history has surely disproved is that it is better in politics 'to be feared than to be loved'.

Europe lags behind the USA in its conviction and enthusiasm of response to a shared Western decline. President Obama may have disappointed on many fronts. But his administration compares to Europe as the poetry of opportunity stands to the prose of despondency. We might do well to recall George Bernard Shaw's well-worn advice that 'The possibilities are numerous once we decide to act and not react.' There is good reason to believe that a Europe in relative decline can remain the author of its own fate. But to do so it needs to redirect many of its economic and strategic policies and show a greater capability to learn the lessons of previous moments of crisis. The consequences of his fellow Romans discarding Marcus Aurelius's rally to strategic level-headedness should be well remembered.

Appendix

References to academic sources have deliberately been kept to a minimum throughout the book. However, the foregoing account draws extensively on a wide range of the author's refereed academic books and articles. For those wishing to explore issues related to European foreign policy from a more academic perspective, the author's recent relevant publications include:

Europe's Role in Global Politics: A Retreat from Liberal Internationalism, Routledge, 2010.
European Democracy Promotion: A Critical Global Assessment, Johns Hopkins University Press, 2010. Edited.
Energy Security: Europe's New Foreign Policy Challenge, Routledge, 2009.
Democracy's New International Challenges, Routledge, 2009. Edited, with Peter Burnell.
'The end of the Euro-Mediterranean vision', *International Affairs,* 85/5, 2009. With Kristina Kausch.
'Democracy as external governance?', *Journal of European Public Policy,* 16/6, 2009.
'The EU and Ukraine: a door neither open nor closed', *International Politics,* 46/4, 2009.

'Fusing security and development: another Euro-platitude?',
    Journal of European Integration, 30/3, 2008.
'Trends in democracy assistance: what is Europe doing?',
    Journal of Democracy, 19/2, 2008.
'Europe and the Gulf: strategic neglect', *Studia Diplomatica*,
    LX, 2007. With Ana Echagüe.
Europe and the Middle East: In the Shadow of September 11,
    Lynne Reinner, 2006.
*International Democracy and the West: The Role of
    Governments, NGOs and Multinationals*, Oxford
    University Press, 2004.
*The European Union and the Promotion of Democracy:
    Europe's Mediterranean and East Asian Policies*, Oxford
    University Press, 2002.

Index

Page numbers followed by 'n' refer to footnotes.